Get A **FREE** Paperback Copy Of Mitche's Best-Selling Book That Revolutionized The Customer Experience!

Get your FREE paperback at www.PowerMarketing101.com/CS

Download Your Copy of Mitche's FREE Report "5 Steps To Digital Detox"

Visit
www.PowerMarketing101.com/detox

© 2024 Mitche Graf.

All rights reserved. No part of this publication may be reproduced, stored in a retrieval system, or transmitted in any form or by any means, electronic, mechanical, photocopying, recording or otherwise, without the written prior permission of the author.

Cover Design: Muhammad Majid
Editor: Michelle Morgan
Publisher: GrafCorp International, LLC
P.O. Box 405
Aurora, Oregon 97002 USA

Available in Paperback, Hardcover, Kindle & Audiobook

FOR BULK ORDERS OR GROUP DISCOUNTS
CALL: 888.719.4692

Paperback

ISBN: 979-8-9855833-2-8

DEDICATION

This book is dedicated to my two wonderful teenage children, Jaycee (age 19) and Colton (age 17), who were born into a generation where devices are a part of their anatomy. Since the the world has been overcome with the "digital diarrhea" bug, it has convinced me that I want something better for myself, my kids, and the world. Jaycee and Colton, I want to let you both know that I love you, and I would give my life for you. Now, put down that freakin' phone and tell me how your day was!

Dad

Table of Contents

FOREWORD i

INTRODUCTION viii

Chapter-1 : Sky Dragons & Secret Gardens 1

Chapter-2 : Parenting in the Age of Cell Phones 6

Chapter-3 : The Unseen Leash: Are You a Smartphone Puppet? 14

Chapter-4 : Phantom Buzzes and Ghostly Pings: The Haunting of the Modern Mind 28

Chapter-5 : Likes, LOLs, and Loneliness: The Social Media Soup 42

Chapter-6 : The Never-Ending Workday: Thanks, Smartphone 52

Chapter-7 : Appy Ever After? The Myth of Productivity Apps .. 64

Chapter 8 : The 7-Day Digital Detox Plan 74

Chapter-9 : Screen Time to Scream Time: The Fatal Cost of Mobile Multitasking 96

Chapter-10 : Lifestyle Design 108

Chapter-11 : Effective Time Management 162

Chapter-12 : It's A Wrap 178

FOREWORD

The first time I heard the catch phrase, "Addiction is not a moral failing", I was on a journey to discover how best to support adolescents in recovery from substance use disorder (SUD). Otherwise understood as the grip of addiction, the acronym, SUD, suggests the concept that we all can use alcohol or other drugs (or cell phones) if we want to, but that some of us are hardwired or compelled to use them in ways that cause harm to ourselves or others. Be it alcohol, food, drugs, fast cars, exercise or **digital despair with cell phone in hand**, addiction takes many forms.

That one phrase, "Addiction is not a moral failing," was a refrain often used by United States Surgeon General, Vivek Murthy, as he introduced the nation to his report on alcohol, drugs and health in 2016.[1] When I heard those words, it was a reaffirmation that I wasn't the problem. Instead, the big problem was the way **alcohol** affected me. It removed shame.

The idea that I'm hardwired to behave in certain ways that are detrimental to my well-being flies in the face of the American notion that we are all on a journey of manifest destiny. "I should be able to control this! I am in charge of myself. Why can't I control this?!"

"If only I work hard enough, and plan and execute sufficiently, the world will be mine!" This is what we were told at a young age. If we're "tough enough", we won't need any help. In fact, the lack of harmony present in the statement alone should suggest the danger of such a conquering mindset.

As an educational leader in long-term recovery, I understand the dangers of addiction in more than one way. I've experienced the freedom one can find living in recovery, and I've cried upon hearing the news of an adolescent's premature death caused by addiction, be it alcohol, drugs or texting while driving.

I know first-hand the self-preservation benefits that accompany recovery-oriented behaviors, and being glued to our smart-devices is not one of those. In fact, like all other self-soothing behaviors human beings engage in as they seek to relieve stress or avoid life on life's terms, digital consumption is one of the most **insidious** of addictive behaviors. How could our cell phone kill us? Or hurt those we love?

The phrase "substance use disorder" is insufficient for capturing the breadth of dangers surrounding the human condition when it comes to the over-consumption of things that might otherwise be beneficial in smaller doses. Because, in the end, many things **can kill if used or taken in excess**. Moderation can be a key for some, and for many, it is not possible without a solution. **Mitche Graf provides solutions.**

Graf's pragmatic offering of self-preservation strategies will give you confidence as you work to manage life without the self-soothing **distraction of the device**. Not only might it help you manage life and bring you serenity each day, it just might also **save your life**.

I strongly encourage you to read this book with a close friend. There is a volume of research on addiction and recovery. We know that walking a pathway of behavior change is best done with others. Positive role models make the difference. Others wanting to rid themselves of the

dangers of the device can hold you gently accountable to your own goals.

Taking this digital moderation journey alone, like any recovery journey, is likely to fail if we do it without the help of others... if we try to go it alone. In fact, in his most recent declarations on health risks, Surgeon General Murthy made it clear our nation is experiencing a depth of despair brought on and accompanied by loneliness.[2] The health risks of **loneliness** and the desperation it brings with it are amplified by the loneliness our children feel when we love our device more than we love the time we get to spend with them.

Mitche Graf provides a robust and tangible set of solutions for ***digital moderation***. Read it once. Read it twice. Take his suggestions to heart and apply them in your life. You will find peace and serenity at the end of the day. In the end, it will be clear to you that what really mattered in life were not the email responses or the brief moments of laughter watching Tik-Tok. ***What really matters in life are the relationships you will foster when your device is tucked away***.

Tony Mann, D.Ed.

1. U.S. Department of Health and Human Services. (2016). *Facing addiction in America: The Surgeon General's report on alcohol, drugs and health*. Washington, D.C. U.S. Department of Health and Human Services, Office of the Surgeon General.

2. The US Surgeon General's Advisory on the Healing Effects of Social Connection and Community. (2023). *Our Epidemic of Loneliness and Isolation*. Washington, D.C. U.S. Department of Health and Human Services, Office of the Surgeon General.

About Your Captain For This Flight

Mitche Graf has been a lifestyle entrepreneur for over 35 years and has launched more businesses than some people have hot dinners, He has shown he's got the Midas touch for turning ideas into gold.

From hawking lemonade in the 3rd grade to selling bikes out of his garage in the 7th grade, Mitche has always been a business whiz kid. These days, he's running three companies, and plans on adding to an impressive tally of 12 businesses he's scaled and sold.

He also took a year off from running his own companies to be the President of a Class A affiliate of the world-champion San Francisco Giants. In 2019, he led an organizational re-brand that had fans pouring in, boosting attendance by 12%, one of the largest increased in all of professional baseball.

Mitche has launched multiple award-winning restaurants, a bustling catering and events company, a national spice manufacturing business, an award-winning photography studio, and even a night crawler company. Because, why not? He's also founded a national cribbage board company, an award-winning limousine business, a portable hot tub rental service, a drive-through espresso company, an educational products company, and an athletic fitness testing corporation.

As a radio host, Mitche's voice can be heard on *"The Business Edge Minute"* and *"The BBQ Radio Show,"* which air on over 100 radio stations nationwide. His quick wit and fast-paced style have made his shows hit the top 1.5% of all podcasts as well, earning them significant national press.

Mitche is also an international best-selling author. He's penned 10 books, covering everything from marketing espresso to unleashing your inner ninja. His titles include:

- "Marketing Your Espresso Business" (1994)
- "Power Marketing, Selling & Pricing" (2004) - Best Seller
- "The Passionate Life: A Common Man's Dream To Getting Anything You Want Out Of Everything You Do" (2009)
- "The Unleashed Entrepreneur: A KickAss Guide To Harnessing Your Inner Ninja, Working Less, & Building The Lifestyle Of Your Dreams" (2018) - Best Seller
- "BBQ Unleashed Recipe Book" (2018)
- "High Voltage Branding: Go from Ordinary to Extra-Ordinary" (2020)
- "The Business Basics BootCamp: The Ultimate Crash Course" (2020) - Best Seller
- "Entertain Like a Pro: Appetizers" (2020)
- "Customer Service Is DEAD: Delivering 6-Star Service in A 1-Star World" (2021)
- "Snuggles, Kisses & Hugs Have a Party" (written with his 7-year-old daughter Sierra)

He has taught his high-voltage seminars and workshops to

over 105,000 people in nine countries and nearly every U.S. state (sorry, Maine!). He's earned his PhD from The School of Hard Knocks, with a major in "Getting Punched in the Face by Failure." His failures have been his best teachers, but he's always come back swinging. From his business highs to bankruptcy in the early 90's, Mitche has always fought tooth and nail to carve out a niche for himself, regardless of what industry he was dabbling in at the time.

When he's not revolutionizing the business world, Mitche is all about work-life balance. He loves the outdoors, playing guitar, cooking, enjoying good wine, and spending quality time with his family. He volunteers as the PA Announcer for five varsity sports at the local high school, and in his free time, you might find him fishing, gold panning, gardening, telling bad jokes, or writing songs.

Living in a small town in Oregon, Mitche is the proud daddy to three incredible kids, Jaycee, Colton, and Sierra. His household also includes dogs Tilly and Delilah, a lizard named Opa, and several hundred guppies (names not important). His motto is "work less, live more," so he can focus on what truly matters. For Mitche, every day is a Saturday.

For speaking inquiries, please contact All American Speakers Bureau (www.AllAmericanSpeakers.com) or call 888-719-4692.

Mitche can lecture on a vast plethora of topics including delivering 6-star customer service, entrepreneurship, starting a business, branding, marketing, time management, lifestyle design, work/life balance, motivation, selling a business, and controlling social media.

INTRODUCTION

Homework? Before the book even gets to chapter 1?

ABSOLUTELY!

Before we begin our wonderful journey together, I'm going to give you a very short homework assignment. Right now, go to your phone's settings, then click on Screen Time and do these three things-

1- Write down how many hours you have been on your phone today, and what your daily average has been for the past week.
2- Scroll down to the list that shows where you are spending the most time and write down the first 5 apps, which will probably be over 90% of your daily activity.
3- Write down how many daily "pickups" you have, along with the top 3 categories.

Right now, you are thinking one of two things- You are either saying to yourself, *"What, what? There's no way I spend that much time on my phone"*, or *"Phew, I thought that it would be much higher than that?"* If you picked option 2, you are a big fat liar and must spend the next 10 minutes without your phone.

We will revisit these numbers later, but for now, just put them on your kitchen fridge for safe keeping.

Being born at the tail end of the Baby Boom generation,

there wasn't any Internet for me to waste my time on. There were no cell phones, no computer games, no social media, and no endless streaming services to suck my time.

If we wanted to do something we took a ball outside and played catch, kicked a tin can around the parking lot, or rode our skateboards around the neighborhood. Our mothers rang the dinner bell when it was time to eat, we ate, then we went back outside to play some more before it was time for our showers and bed. If a good show was on TV, we would sit in the living room as a family and watch it together. We would laugh together, cry together, pop some popcorn on the stove (microwaves weren't a "thing" yet), laugh some more, then the TV went off.

There was no such thing as leaving the TV on in the background just because... It just didn't happen.

Most families had one TV...if you had two TV's, you were considered upper crust. Fancy. Snooty. The nerve of some people.

I remember there only being 4 channels to watch- NBC, ABC, CBS, and PBS. That was it! Today, there are literally thousands of options for what to watch, and everything is available at our fingertips.

Dinner used to be an occasion for catching up with each other and hearing about our days, talking about what we were going to do on the weekend, and maybe even play a family game. Yes, I said play a family game...TOGETHER!

If you are too young to remember times like this, I bet you have been told many stories by your parents or other relatives about the 'good ole days.'

The reality is that things have changed, and they will never go back to the way they were. Some say that's good; some say they will never give in to the siren's call of technology.

Regardless of what side of the fence you come down on, we all must admit that our cell phones have literally taken over every aspect of our lives to the point that they have crept into just about every nook and cranny, with or without our permission.

We wake up on the morning, we check our phone.
We eat breakfast, with our phone in our face.
We have nothing to do, so we pick up our phone.
We go to the restroom, yep, you guessed it.
We take a lunch break, first thing we do is check our phone.
We eat dinner, we are on our phone.
We go to bed, we take our phone with us and fall asleep with it on our chest.

In fact, an average American picks up their cell phone 144 times a day, and averages nearly 4 hours and 30 minutes each day with a device in their face. If you figure that you are sleeping 8 hours a day, it simply means you are spending about 30% of your awake time looking down.

I have to admit that I love my phone. I get all of my news, sports scores, weather, school grades, recipes, and stupid cat videos from it. This is both a wonderful advantage and av curse. It seems that all the time that I now spend scrolling used to be used doing something else more productive.

Where did all this time come from? Something had to give. There's not a magical 25th hour in the day that mysteriously appears in your schedule. It came from time with your family, time with your friends, time with yourself.

Does this sound like anyone you know? Don't feel bad, you are not alone in this addiction. Most of the modern world has fallen prey to the call of the screen, but I'm here to tell you that it's not too late to come to a screeching halt, reset your thinking, and create new patterns and habits. That's what this book is about, giving you the tools to take the digital dragon by the horn and get back control over your time, and in many cases your life!

Let me ask you a simple question.

What would you do with an extra 30 minutes every day to do with whatever you wanted? Would you spend that time with your children, with your spouse, with your best friend? Would you take that time and invest it into your own personal education?

Possibly donate that time to your favorite charity, invest it into growing a business, or visiting an old friend? Or maybe just spending that time sitting on your back deck enjoying a little bit of peace and quiet with a good cuppa coffee?

What would you do with an extra hour every single day? What about 2 hours more each and every day to make a difference in your life...and the lives of the people that mean the most to you.

If you ask people what their biggest problem is today, I venture to say that a majority of us would say that we just don't have enough time in the day to get the things done that we want. With all of the chaos and craziness in the world right now, it seems like we are busier than ever, but we seem to get less and less done. We each have 86,400 seconds in our days, and we can't create any more of it. There's not a 25th hour that we can magically make appear.

I want to share a story before we begin that will hopefully set the stage for the journey we are about to embark on.

Once upon a time, a big, strong woodcutter got a job working for a local business. The pay was great and so were the benefits.

The woodcutter was excited and determined to do his absolute best to impress the boss. His boss gave him an axe and showed him the area where he was to work.

On the first day, the woodcutter brought back twenty-five trees. *"That's great,"* said the boss. *"Keep up the good work!"*

Totally motivated by his boss's encouragement, the woodcutter tried even harder the second day, but he could only bring back fifteen trees. On the third day, he only brought back ten trees. Day after day, he kept bringing back fewer and fewer. Something's wrong with me, the woodcutter surmised. I'm losing my strength.

He went to the boss and apologized, saying he could not understand what was going on. *"When was the last time you sharpened your axe?"* asked the boss. *"Sharpened my axe? I don't have time; I've been too busy cutting down trees!"*

This book is about helping you keep your edge sharp. It's quite easy to get caught up in the "cutting down of trees" and forget to continue to sharpen our axe so that the forest is easier to navigate. I can tell you for 100% certainty that spending countless hours on your device will NOT keep the edge of your sword sharp.

I'm excited to spend some time with you, and I hope you are

just as excited to immerse yourself in making your life the best it can be, and to gain control over your device usage instead of it controlling you.

The journey you are about to take has the potential to change your life forever.

The only thing in this world that we can control is how we spend our time, and if you desire to attain your goals and live the life that you were meant to live, you MUST learn to control that thing in your hand. Period.

Experienced. Practical. Unconventional. Modern.

Not bound by formalities. Eager to pass my experience on to you. My goal for this book is simple: To help you reset your thinking, and to release the creative juices that are inside of you to the point that you become a force unlike anything this world has ever seen.

How about we insert the coin and press play

CHAPTER 1

Sky Dragons & Secret Gardens

Once upon a sunny afternoon, 5-year-old Princess Sierra and her dad, Sir Dad the Great, embarked on their favorite backyard adventure...Forest!

Princess Sierra, in her glittering blue cape, and Sir Dad, in his trusty Dodgers cap, were ready to face the Maripolds and Hollihops. Sierra wielded a sparkling hand-engraved magic wand, while Dad brandished an stick as his mighty sword.

"Our invisibility fields are up!" Sierra announced, waving her wand to activate the imaginary shield around them.

"To the Dragon's Nest!" Sir Dad declared, pointing to the old rope swing they'd transformed into their sanctuary.

The backyard became a fantastical realm. The Maripolds, worm-like creatures with dragon heads, slithered from behind the garden gnomes. The Hollihops, sneaky birds that could dive into the ground, popped up near the flowerbeds. As they approached, Sir Dad suddenly stumbled, narrowly avoiding the sprinkler, which they had dubbed "The Fountain of Doom."

"Quick, use your magic wand, Princess Sierra!" Dad urged, doing a dramatic spin that nearly made him trip over Miss Tilly & Miss Delilah, their dogs, who decided to join in the fun and games.

Sierra giggled, pointing her wand at the Maripolds. *"Rainbow beam, activate!"* she shouted, sending the imaginary enemies retreating with colorful, invisible blasts.

They ran toward the Dragon's Nest, dodging Hollihops that leapt from behind bushes. Sierra's laughter echoed through the yard, her eyes sparkling with delight. Reaching the swing, Dad lifted her up, declaring, *"We need help, and we need it fast!"*

Just then, an entire flock of Sky Dragons appeared on the horizon, just in time to scare off a majority of the bad guys, and Sir Dad & Princess Sierra greeted them with huge waves and hoorays! The few remaining Maripolds disappeared around the house, and they were safe once more.

They collapsed on the grass, breathless and happy. Sierra looked up at the sky, imagining dragons soaring among the clouds. *"Dad, do you think the Sky Dragons can live with us all the time?"*

Sir Dad. *"Absolutely my baby angel. Then we can play with them whenever we want. We have to keep our imagination alive every day, so I think it's a great idea that they stay with us always."*

Sierra nodded thoughtfully. *"We have to keep our imagination alive, so they know we're ready if they ever need us."*

Sierra's eyes widened with a new idea. *"Can we visit the Secret Garden next? It's where the Sky Dragons rest!"*

"Lead the way, Princess Sierra," Dad said, standing up with a flourish.

They tiptoed to the far corner of the garden, where the tomatoes and pumpkins grew. Sierra waved her wand, *"Presto chango ishka hobna showota!."* The Secret Garden appeared, filled with blooming flowers and colorful hummingbirds.

Sitting among the blossoms, Dad whispered, *"Sierra, always try to remember these moments. One day, I won't be here to protect you from the Maripolds and Holihops, so you have the promise to always keep your imagination alive. Can you promise me that?"*

Sierra hugged her dad tightly. *"I will, Dad. I promise."*

Sir Dad smiled, eyes misty. *"And next time, we'll bring a snack to the Dragon's Nest, deal?"*

Sierra laughed, *"Can we bring a snack next time for the Sky Dragons, too?"*

"Definitely!" said Sir Dad.

As they lay in the Secret Garden, watching the clouds drift by, looking for shapes in the sky, they knew they had captured a perfect moment.

The adventures, the laughter, and the love—they were all reminders to savor every precious second, making their hearts swell with gratitude and joy. And in that magical backyard, anything was possible, as long as they dreamed and slowed down to enjoy each moment together.

This story is true.

My daughter and I have been playing the game of "Forest" for the past 5+ years, and it all started because I didn't want to miss an opportunity to create a memory for her, and to capture the special moments we shared. In fact, we played a short game last night before bed, even though it was nearly 9:00pm. I just couldn't say no.

The message? We all have our own Sky Dragons in our backyards that we need to remember from time to time. It puts everything in your life in a new perspective and gives you the ability to move mountains for the ones we love.

So, as we begin our journey together, just remember that the special moments in your life are right in from you...you just need to slow down enough to see them.

Which means, put down your freakin' phone!

CHAPTER 2

Parenting in the Age of Cell Phones

I'm old fashioned, I know that without a doubt in the world. I didn't get married for the first time until I was 43, and my first child came out when I was 45. Most of my high school and college buddies have grandchildren that are older than my kids, but the way I look at it I had the chance to live a full life before I settled down and began my family.

There's pros and cons for waiting to have kids, but I do believe it does give you a distinct advantage when it comes to raising kids...you've been able to watch how everyone else did it, so you will have a better idea of what to do with your owns cherubs.

Waiting gave me more patience, more understanding of what is right and wrong, and a keener sense of how I wanted to raise my own kids.

It makes me cringe when I see 4 and 5-year-old toddlers sitting in the corner playing on a phone or iPad. There is no way in heaven that a child that young should be given a phone for unlimited time, under any circumstance.

Occasionally, I get. But to give a little human a device to act as a babysitter is probably the unhealthiest thing you could ever do to your own flesh and blood. Their brains and bodies can't handle it, they are not able to control their urges, and they can't understand why too much is a bad thing.

Hey, we all have done it. We are going into a meeting and need an instant babysitter for a few minutes, or we visit a friend and need some quiet time so we toss the kids a bone. But just like everything else, it needs to be in serious doses of moderation.

If you are in the habit of letting your kids play endlessly on a device, it's time to rethink your approach.

I have a single piece of advice for you, STOP!

Your most important job as a mother or father is to keep them safe and give them the proper tools to be able to be successful in life. Striking that delicate balance is definitely a big challenge but is one that needs your complete attention.

The Age Dilemma: When Should Kids Get Their First Cell Phone?

That's the $64,000 question. There's no one-size-fits-all

answer, but here's a rule of thumb: if your child still believes in the Tooth Fairy, it might be a tad early. Generally speaking, a large number of experts suggest waiting until at least middle school, around the ages 11-13, when kids start becoming more independent and responsible.

Even at this age, their brains are not completely developed and have difficulty determining what is right and wrong, and what appropriate behavior is. Again, there's no hard-and-fast rule, it all depends on a variety of factors that only you and your family can determine.

Giving a young child some sort of device too early can lead to some very serious consequences. Younger kids are like baby puppies—they get distracted easily, and a constant barrage of notifications doesn't help. You are a full-blown adult, and you know how difficult it is for you to control the urges, so how can you expect a young child to control those urges? That's easy, they can't!

Your children also need to learn how to properly interact with real people, not just avatars on a screen. The socialization that we all lost during COVID had dramatic effects on the mental health of our entire society, and I believe that we are still dealing with many of the ramifications from that period of time.

There's also the increased risk of cyberbullying. Younger kids are more vulnerable online, and they might not have the maturity to handle a mean comment or online predators. Giving them a phone too early is like sending them into a jungle with a raw steak tied to their back.

A study at the University of California at San Francisco

showed that the more time kids spend using a screen from ages 9 to 11, the higher their odds of suicidal behavior two years later. In fact, each additional hour of screen time a day brings with it an increased risk of suicide by 9%. That fact alone should shake you to your soul.

Simple Tips For Helping Control Screen Usage

I could spend hours talking about how we, as parents, are letting the younger generation down by normalizing cell phone usage, but instead will simply give you some pointers on things you can do to help limit how much time your child spends on a device.

1. Set Screen Time Schedules

Create a screen time schedule like it's a prized TV slot. Prime time only after their homework is completed to your satisfaction, chores, and a dose of good ol' fresh air.

2. Digital Curfews

Think of it as tucking in their devices with a bedtime story. *"Goodnight, iPhone 15 Pro Max. I hope you dream of low battery alerts and Roblox."*

3. Tech-Free Zones

Declare certain areas of your home tech-free zones. I recommend the dinner table for sure, and perhaps the living room when you have 'family movie night." If you are going to watch a movie together, WATCH A MOVIE TOGETHER!

4. Activity Swap

How about swapping some screen time for other activities. One hour of Dungeons & Dragons equals one hour of playing an actual sport, outdoors!

5. Device Hotels

I have some friends that do this, and I think it's genius! When you go into their home, you put your phone in a basket until you leave.. We do something similar when we have some sort of party at our house, where there are signs that say 'NO DEVICE ZONE' throughout the house. It actually works, and people enjoy themselves more because they are more engaged in conversations. Give it a try at your next dinner party!

6. App Limits

It's very simple to set daily limits on their devices so that they can't spend unlimited time with their head buried.

7. Screen Time as Currency

Chores and homework can earn minutes of screen time. Spend 1 hour cleaning your room, you get 30 minutes of Minecraft.

8. Family Screen Time Rules

This is a tough one. Lead by example and show them that even adults have screen limits. This will be difficult if you yourself spend all day swiping up, but necessary.

9. Weekly Screen Detox

Sundays are for family picnics, board games, and face-to-face conversations. It's the perfect day to turn off all devices and focus on being present for your family.

10. Reward System

Extra screen time can be earned for good behavior, completed chores, turned in homework, and exceptional acts of kindness.

Bonus Tip: Humor and Creativity

You can also use humor and creativity to enforce these rules. 'Today's Wi-Fi password is hidden in this riddle: What runs but never walks, has a mouth but never talks, has a bed but never sleeps? Solve it, and the internet is yours for 1 hour!

These are all merely suggestions on creative ways to help your child minimize their screen time, and I'm sure you can come up with your own list that is specific to your parenting style. The point is, do SOMETHING!

The Young Parent Conundrum

Being a young parent in the digital age has its own unique set of challenges. You're often balancing a career, your personal life, and the pressure of raising tech-savvy kids. The generational tech gap today is very real. You might struggle to keep up with the ever-evolving tech trends that your kids are naturally adept at.

Younger parents might feel pressured to conform to what other parents are doing, leading to early tech exposure for their kids. Remember, just because Little Johnny down the street has a phone at 7, doesn't mean it's right for your kid. Stand firm in your decisions and do what's best for your family.

Finding Your Balance

I believe that this is the most difficult time to raise a kid that the world has ever seen, and unfortunately, there's no easy answers on how to safely do it. Coming up with an approach that makes sense for your family is uniquely yours, and nobody else can dictate what to do.

Just remember that parenting is a long journey, and not a destination. There will be bumps and potholes along the way, but each challenge is an opportunity to teach, learn, and grow.

CHAPTER 3

The Unseen Leash: Are You a Smartphone Puppet?

It's a beautiful summer Sunday morning. The birds are chirping, as the sun does its best impression of a Broadway star, with a gentle breeze whispering "It's a perfect day." You're sitting at your favorite café, sipping on what the barista confidently called "the best latte you'll ever have." Across from you, your friend is recounting a story about how a snake was eating his goldfish from his outdoor pond. But here's the twist – you're not really listening. Why? Because your phone just buzzed, and in your mind that is much more important.

In the middle of this almost cinematic perfection, your attention isn't on your friend's tale but on that 5.5-inch screen. Congratulations, you've just been puppeteered by your smartphone!

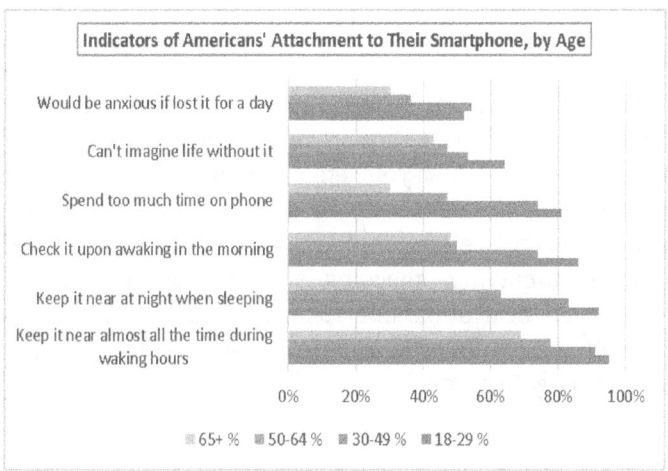

Source GALLUP:
https://news.gallup.com/poll/393785/americans-close-wary-bond-smartphone.aspx

In this idyllic setting, where life seems to be a series of picture-perfect moments, our story can take an unexpected turn. The buzz of your phone becomes the modern-day siren's call that lures you away from the world's natural splendors and the warmth of human interaction. This isn't just a tale of distraction but a glimpse into a powerful force that's reshaping our behaviors and interactions. And the puppeteer behind this transformation is a neurotransmitter called dopamine.

Dopamine: The Science of Screen Addiction

Imagine your brain as a personal cheer squad, complete with pom-poms and spirited chants. Every time you interact with your phone, this squad goes wild, cheering you on. Each notification, like, or message is a metaphorical high-five, releasing dopamine, the brain's feel-good neurotransmitter. It's like nature's way of giving you a thumbs-up, encouraging a repeat performance.

But here's the catch. This dopamine-driven feedback loop is more cunning than a fox in a henhouse. It starts off harmlessly – a peek at your emails, a quick scroll through social media, a short reply to a text your mother sent yesterday. And before you know it, it spirals into an unrelenting craving, checking your phone morphs into seeking that next dopamine rush. It's a cycle that clamps onto you like a stubborn barnacle, constantly hungering for the next ping, buzz, or ring.

> **Random Fact:** Gen Z is the most inclined to check their phones within 5 minutes after receiving a notification (Dove Recovery, 2023) (ATC Columbus).

The Complicated Relationship with Your Phone

Your phone is like that friend who always has the juiciest gossip – you can't help but pay attention. It showers you with attention, keeps you in the loop, and never runs out of new tricks. But, like any high-maintenance relationship, it demands a lot from you – your time, focus, and often, your sanity.

It is a master at the art of pickpocketing your time; one minute you're checking the weather, and the next thing you know, an hour has vanished into thin air while you watch videos of a honey badger eating a snake, or a skateboarder falling off the roof of a building.

Like a cunning magician, your phone is an expert at misdirection. It steals your attention from the real world, leaving you to juggle between the virtual and the actual.

In its quest for your attention, your phone often hijacks your peace of mind. Each beep and buzz can bring anything, ranging from a smile to a surge of stress.

Here's usually how it works:

- **The Hook:** It begins with a simple notification – a 'like' on your photo or a comment on your reel. It feels good, right? It's a digital pat on the back.
- **The Line:** Gradually, you start expecting these pats. You find yourself glancing at your phone more often, waiting for the next hit of digital approval.
- **The Sinker:** Now, you're deep in the loop. Your phone becomes the first thing you check in the morning and the last thing at night. You're hooked, line, and sinker.

The False Sense of Connection

There's an illusion your phone creates by convincing you

that you're connected when, in fact, you may be isolated. It's like being at a party and surrounded by people, but not really engaging with anyone. Your phone provides this constant stream of updates, likes, and messages, giving you the impression that you're connected to a larger world. But let's peel back this digital veneer.

The interactions on your phone are often shallow, like skimming the surface of a lake without ever diving in. You might have hundreds of friends on social media, but how many can you call to come through for you in the middle of the night during a crisis?

It is necessary to evaluate the quality of these digital acquaintances. Do they make your life better, or are you just trading shallow experiences? Real friendship is not about the number but the quality of the friends you have. They are those which require physical presence and face-to-face communication where you can notice the non-verbal cues, hear the intonation and get a full interaction with the other party.

Have you ever been somewhere, maybe at school, work, home, or even out with friends, but you are not connecting with them mentally? This scenario can be said to be a false impression of linkage, which explains that you can be physically present at a place, but not really living in the moment or engaging with anyone.

> **Random Fact:** 36% of Millennials claim to look at their smartphones for personal activities for at least 2 hours each workday (Enterprise Apps Today, 2023) (Enterprise Apps Today).

The Irony of Choice

Your phone is like a digital buffet that you have access to 24/7... apps, games, and social media. It seems to give peculiarity and emancipation, and yet it results in an affection of discomfort and reluctance – the curse of obtainable options. Here is how it plays out:

Due to the data overload, the decision-making process is more difficult when you are shown many alternatives to choose from. It is like standing in front of your refrigerator trying to make a decision on what to eat. Do you eat the pizza from last Friday night, or perhaps the leftover casserole from who-knows-when?

While having an array of alternatives is often intended as a good thing, it may result in doubt in your decision-making, asking whether you made the right decision or if there is something better somewhere else. This can lead to an extended state of unhappiness and FOMO (Fear of Missing Out).

You already know that you can do better when you just concentrate on the essentials or when you just clean up the mental plate that you are serving from too many distractions.

However, the key above all is in moderating what you decide to tap into on the phone. It's more about the worth of the content that is being produced rather than the amount of content. A relevant question to ask is: does this app, game, or social media platform make my life better? Am I getting the feeling of elation, am I running down, or am I feeling a bit low? Subsequently, being selective can assist you in not falling prey to the paradox of choice, which makes your digital experience more satisfying.

> **Random Fact:** Gen Z is the generation most likely to experience anxiety after losing their phone (Dove Recovery, 2023) (ATC Columbus).

The Mirage of Multitasking

When I was younger, I considered myself an expert multitasker. I prided myself on being able to simultaneously juggle up to 8 tasks at a time, while still being able to complete them on time. But what I learned was that I was only short-changing myself because I wasn't able to give 100% to each task. This meant that everything was done with mediocrity.

Multitasking has become the new status symbol in society, especially in the high-tech society that we live in today. To a large extent, our phones, these sleek little wonders, have made us believe in the illusion of multitasking. Through our phones, we can confirm our gym appointment for tomorrow, check the scores, and even surf a recipe website for tonight's dessert, all at the same time.

You can picture yourself in the kitchen trying to whip up a batch of your world-famous meatloaf, bust a move to your favorite Taylor Swift song on Alexa, and, just for kicks, solve a complex algebra problem.

Sound chaotic? That's because it really is. The truth is we do all of these with our phones every day by juggling multiple tasks in a futile attempt to be productive. But here's the kicker; it's a mirage.

There is no such thing as multi-tasking, but task-switching.

Multitasking with your phone is like trying to watch a movie while reading a book and having a meaningful conversation all at the same time. Sure, you're doing three things at once, but you are not really absorbing or enjoying any of them.

Research has shown time and time again that when we split our attention, we're not giving our best to any task. Our brains are not wired to focus on multiple complex tasks at the same time. What we're really doing is task-switching, rapidly shifting our focus from one thing to another, and each switch comes with a cost.

This cost is what I like to call the 'efficiency burn.' Every time you switch tasks, there's a little lag, a tiny moment where your brain has to shift gears. These moments add up, chipping away at your productivity and efficiency. Well, it is like having a car that stalls at every traffic signal – it never reaches its full speed.

You have to wonder about the quality of work that is produced in this multitasking environment because when you divide your attention, you increase the chances of making a mistake, perhaps a very costly one. In the world of work, this results in lower quality work and increased errors, which often takes more time to accomplish a single task.

What about your creativity? True creativity requires something extremely scarce in today's digital world – mental breathing room, something that I don't think most of us get on a regular basis.

My favorite place on this planet is in Montana in the middle of the Cabinet Mountains. No people, no cell service, no traffic, just the sound of a river meandering by and a joyful noise coming from the variety of birds singing at you.

Did I mention no people and no cell service?

Whenever I've had a rough day, or just need to mentally escape for a few minutes, I envision myself sitting next to that river with a good cup of coffee, staring at the water as it passes by.

Magically, my stress melts away and I am able to see things much more clearly. I've made many important life decisions sitting next to that river, both literally and figuratively. From where we live, it's about a 9-hour drive to get to this heavenly place, so it's not everyday when I can visit. But in my mind, I'm there just about every day of the year.

I can honestly say that I truly look forward to my in-person visits to Montana, because I know I will not have access to the world via my device, and that thought brings me a small amount of stress, but mostly brings me happiness.

If you knew you weren't going to have access to the Internet for 24 hours, how would that make you feel?

For most of my adult life, I have chosen to not just focus on one thing. I've always been involved with many, many activities at the same time. My brain gets bored easily and it must constantly be engaged in several creative activities in order to keep my mojo functioning at a high level.

I have been able to accomplish this by learning to become a master at time-blocking or time-chunking. I call it the POD system, where I block out X amount of time for a particular task and stay diligent to that. I dive into this in great detail in my bonus chapter "Effective Time Management" towards the end of this book.

If you look at my calendar (I use a combo of the old-fashioned written schedule book, and a digital version), you will see a series of boxed out time slots for each day. I only check emails/texts 3 times a day and try to make it a habit to turn off all notifications after 4pm each day.

You can ask anyone in my family about how frustrating it is for them to send me a text, but I don't respond until my next scheduled time to do so. If I did respond to every notification I received in real time during the day while I was trying to accomplish something else, I would venture to say that I would never accomplish ANYTHING!

It may seem that I'm busier than most people, but I also have time to get my 10-year-old on the bus for school and be there when she gets off the bus (I have done this for all my children throughout their school years). I spend time daily in my garden playing in the mud, I play guitar, I read a ton, shop/prepare the family meals, watch every game that my kids are involved in, I make time for my two very energetic dogs who require a lot of balls to be thrown for them daily, and spend time daily on my back deck doing...nothing.

Am I successful 100% of the time? Not even close! It's a daily grind trying to make sure I have the proper balance between my professional and personal lists of to-do's, and the only way I am able to find that balance is to NOT be on my phone all day long and NOT pretend that I'm accomplishing 5 things at once. Seems simple, yet it takes a tremendous amount of discipline to resist falling prey to my device.

Let's imagine that your mind is a garden that you need to take care of properly to make it productive. Ideas cannot grow without space to develop; they require fertile ground in order to grow and mature. They require a state of mind that is free from the interference of the weeds of distraction and the pests of constant notification. With multitasking – in a work environment that becomes a chaotic field of battle – creativity is left to fight for its existence while using a phone as the main weapon.

These moments have one thing in common, and that is the fact that they are moments where the mind is not divided into various tasks. This calm is the soil that creativity grows from, free from the tug of a phone's presence.

Furthermore, multitasking on your phone is a myth that not only hinders creativity but also learning and knowledge retention. If the attention is divided, then the cerebral activity for the storage and processing of information is also divided. It is as productive as trying to collect rainwater in a colander or a mesh – impossible and ultimately, pointless.

In modern time, it seems that we have the attention span of a fly, maybe even less. Studies have shown that the average attention span of an adult is about 7 seconds, which explains why people can go through an entire meal without glancing at their phones at least a dozen times!

> **Random Fact:** 58.5% of Gen Zers reported upgrading their device in the past year, compared to only 43% of Boomers and Gen X (Dove Recovery, 2023) (ATC Columbus).

Action Plan:

1. **Digital Awareness Exercise:** Select a day to be aware of how many times you snatch your phone. When the urge arises, resist it and say, "No, it is not necessary." The question is, why am I compelled to check it? Could it be out of sheer boredom, because it is a routine now, or because I really need to?

2. **Mindful Unplugging:** I recommend that you set some hours of the day where you consciously refrain from having your phone around. It could be before meals, an hour before going to bed, or within an hour after waking up.

3. **Quality Connection Time:** Every single day, set a certain number of hours or minutes during which you can only communicate with a person, for

instance, through a video call or a phone call, with no interruptions of any digital technology.

4. **App Audit:** Check through your phone and delete unwanted applications that are not useful to you in real sense. This clears up your screen and minimizes the distractions that allows you to aimlessly scroll through your feeds.

CHAPTER 4

Phantom Buzzes and Ghostly Pings: The Haunting of the Modern Mind

Pretend that you are in a calm, silent room 'daydreaming' about your summer vacation, or perhaps reading a book. It could begin with that slight tickle at the back of your knee. Subconsciously, your hand automatically slides to your pocket and pulls out your phone, just to discover that there is no call, no text, and no message.

It is the buzz that lies between our ears; the ethereal hum that follows the technological advances that define our current age. This is not merely a peculiar phenomenon, but emblematic of our era and a reflection of how profound the integration of the connection to the digital world into the human existence has become.

I think we're past the point of discussing paranormal events as a concept; this is a real issue that impacts hundreds of millions of people. From the phantom buzz that never occurs to the constant beeps that insist on being noticed, let's learn how our beloved gadgets are rewiring our brains and experiences.

When scrolling through the layers of this digital haunting, we will learn not only about the impact of the constant connection on our psyche and brain but also about the possibility of finding calm amidst the loud digital signals.

The Illusion of Connectivity: Phantom Vibrations Explained

We have all been in a situation where we feel a tickle in our pockets as if there is an insect bite, and we hurriedly grab our phone to check an incoming call only to discover that it is completely off or in vibrate mode.

A phantom vibration is a very similar phenomenon to a mirage, a type of optical illusion that interprets sensory information. In this case, a touch, as a sign that a phone is ringing even if it is not. It mainly happens when the phone is in your pocket or nearby and this creates an impression that a call or message has been received.

> **Random Fact:** 15% of US adults use their smartphones for internet access due to not having broadband at home (Exploding Topics, 2024) (Exploding Topics).

Psychological Explanation

But why does our brain tell such a story? It's because our brains have become meshed with the gadgets we use. It is important to know that we have evolved to have patterns of response to stimuli that are crucial for our existence.

Smartphones are acknowledged as the most significant technological invention of the current generation since they are the center of our social and working lives, as well as being the gateways to entertainment and information. Consequently, our brain defines the smartphone notifications as important stimuli, as the alerts are processed in the same way as environmental threats or opportunities in the history of human evolution.

This is due to the constant expectation of messages and alerts, which contributes to the development of a state of anxiety we feel. This hyper-awareness just means that our brain is much more sensitive to something that would typically go unnoticed.

In essence, our brains are always on high alert, waiting for the next presumed notification to come through. This increases the likelihood of developing a heightened perception of the environment, which may interpret the sensations of the fabric against the skin as a phone vibrating.

As Pavlov trained his dogs to salivate at the sound of a ringing bell which may denote a threat, we train ourselves to tremble as soon as we feel any vibration near our phones because it means a notification has arrived. The conditioning is so powerful that when there is no real alert, our brain creates the sensation for us. It is an illusion that arises from how we expect things to be and so we perceive them in that very way.

> **Random Fact:** 75% of Americans use their phones when using the restroom (Enterprise Apps Today, 2023) ([Enterprise Apps Today](#)).

Case Studies

Studies reveal that a significant number of people do feel these haptic pulsations, with some estimates indicating that as many as 90% of smartphone users have encountered this phenomenon at some point.

The more the phone becomes a part of the user's daily existence, the more the brain prepares itself to wait for an alert, hence, the higher the possibility of imagining their phone vibrating. This steady reoccurrence becomes a vicious circle.

Other study findings include the case of office workers who stated that they experienced a decrease in perceived phantom vibrations when they consciously lowered their phone's ringer or even silenced it. This observation underlines the fact that your brain is very flexible; when the expectation of constant interaction is lowered, there will be less construction of false alarms.

Moreover, the analysis of this phenomenon has also touched upon identifying psychological traits that can predispose a person to these sensations. It was also concluded that people with high levels of anxiety or people who heavily rely on their phones to socialize are the most susceptible to these ghostly buzzes. This means that how we emotionally respond to a situation and interact with our technological gadgets can determine the sensations we get.

Rewiring the Brain: The Effects of Constant Digital Alertness

Neurological Impact

As we enter an era where technology surrounds us in every aspect of our lives, the human brain is not just receiving and analyzing data; it is evolving. It is indeed much more than a distraction; it is a force that is reshaping our brains in many ways through the seemingly innocuous alerts from our smartphones. Every ping, beep, and buzz, not to mention the gentle hum and the constant notification, modify our brain's structure and mechanism.

This particular phenomenon can be best explained through the concept of neuroplasticity, which is the ability of the brain to alter following exposure to certain stimuli. If we rapidly flick between screens and apps to respond to notifications each time, then we are strengthening the neural connections that support attention shifting. This can gradually result in alterations in the structure and function in the prefrontal cortex, which is responsible for attentional control, decision-making processes, and cognitive flexibility. This is quite a flexible approach in the human brain; however, these changes may not always be regarded as positive.

For instance, constantly being a target of notifications from our digital devices can result in a shortening of our attention span, or the amount of information we can hold in our working memory, or even impact our ability to engage in deep and creative thinking. This is where that 7-seconds comes in! We shift our focus more often than a high school boy changes his girlfriend.

However, it also entails the involvement of the brain reward system in this process. The digital alerts that are sent are known to have the ability to release dopamine, which is a feel-good hormone. This makes us constantly wait for that reward of getting likes, messages or new information, thus creating an endless feedback loop.

However, this can make the brain dull to signals that are constant as it needs more stimuli to produce the same amount of dopamine to that of substance addiction.

This is exactly what happens with someone who is addicted to drugs, or alcohol. Their body needs more and more of the substance in order to get the same sensation of being high or drunk. Their tolerance goes up and up over time.

So, whether someone is addicted to drugs, alcohol, cigarettes, or their phone…our brain treats these addictions in the same way. It makes us want MORE!

This desensitization can lead to a general decrease in a person's ability to notice and seek pleasure in less exciting everyday things that could lead to dissatisfaction with our lives and possibly mental illness.

This may explain why so many people seem to not be enjoying their lives yet are content in spending up to ½ of their time with their faces buried in their phone.

Navigating the Digital Maze: Teens, Social Media, and the Quest for Mental Wellness

In our post-COVID world where we all rely on our devices for more information, teens' mental health has become more complex than the tangled wires of my headphones of my childhood Walkman (for those too young to know what a Walkman is, it was a large device that you could clip to your pants that played CD's). Hey, don't laugh, if you had a Walkman, you were considered one of the cool kids!

Let's zoom in on a 2022 article from the high-brow pages of the American Economic Review. Economists, armed with data and probably too much coffee or energy drinks, embarked on an experiment with young adults, aiming to untangle the web of their social media usage.

A whopping 31% of time spent on apps was due to what they elegantly termed "self-control problems."

This discovery fits snugly into the broader narrative of "digital addiction." Picture this: teens scrolling endlessly, with their thumbs moving faster than a cheetah on a treadmill. These same screen-savvy teens rate themselves as less conscientious. They often have parents who are more laissez-faire about screen time than a sloth on a lazy Sunday.

I venture to say that if the parents have the habit of spending all their time on their phone, their kids will think that it's appropriate and will do the same.

These characteristics – the endless scrolling and laid-back parenting – might just be the sneaky culprits behind poor mental health in teens.

Parents need to lead by example, in all areas of life, including how to appropriately use a cell phone.

Now, let's not paint all social media with the same doom-and-gloom brush. It's not the villain twirling its mustache in the shadows. It's more like that friend who's great in small doses but becomes a bit too much after the third hour of non-stop chatting. It's all about moderation – a crucial word in your digital diet.

> **Random Fact:** 87% of smartphone users check their phones less than an hour before going to bed (Exploding Topics, 2024)
> ([Exploding Topics](#))

Interviews/Research

To get a clear picture of the extent of this problem, several scholars in the field of psychology and neuroscience have offered their opinions. Dr. Jane Smith, a cognitive behavior neurologist, explains, *"It is evident that digital technology has taken over our lives in a manner that changes our neural wiring. What we can observe is that there is a direct correlation between the usage of digital devices and a change in brain function and anatomy."*

In a study that was conducted in the Journal of Applied Psychology, it was revealed that the more that people use their smartphones, the more their stress and anxiety levels increase. Individuals in the low-tech group that were required to reduce their use of technology fared better in mental health and cognitive tests.

The study that was conducted at Harvard University involved examining the consequences of continuous notifications on cognition. This study suggested that the participants who received constant alerts performed worse on tasks that demand focus and judgement. The researchers explained that interruptions cause our thinking to be broken up, and this contributes to what the authors referred to as surface learning, which is a shallow way of dealing with information.

Finding Peace: Reducing Digital Noise

Living in the age of constant connectivity that is filled with information is crucial to search for quiet and to minimize digital interference for the sake of your psychological well-being. Basically, you need to find your own 'Montana' wherever you are!

Here are some practical tips on how to reduce the time spent online, real life success stories, and potential advantages of such an approach.

Strategies for Quieting the Mind: Practical Tips for Reducing Digital Interruptions

1. **Take Control of Notifications**: For sanity, it is critical to mute all the notifications that are unnecessary. This simple action could reduce a lot of interruptions in the day and assist people in being able to concentrate more.

2. **Timebox Distractions**: Designate certain hours of the day as 'leisure time' during which one can use their various gadgets. This practice makes certain that these activities do not consume much of the day and assists in increasing efficiency.
3. **Change Your Surroundings**: This is a very good option, as it helps one change their thinking direction or perspective. This approach is supported by psychological literature as it is noted that new environments reduce the negative effects of digital disruptions.
4. **Implement Time-Blocking**: This entails effective planning of your day and dividing it into certain hours and assigning certain tasks to be done during that hour. The goal is to minimize the chances of digital intrusions.
5. **Set Up Email Filters and Rules**: Sort your emails by removing the unwanted ones as they take much space and time to sort. This assist in the management of the email environment as it reduces stress.
6. **Use 'Do Not Disturb' Mode**: Every modern tool that contributes to productivity or our day-to-day activities has a 'Do Not Disturb' feature. Applying this characteristic during the implementation of the deep work concept can help avoid interruptions

from the calls, messages, or notifications on the applications.
7. **Limit Social Media Interaction**: This has the effect of simplifying the social media experience and minimizing the amount of digital noise present. It could be by unfollowing unnecessary accounts and reducing the amount of time spent on social networks so as to concentrate more on other important tasks.
8. **Pomodoro Technique**: Follow the Pomodoro Technique where you work for 25 minutes and then take a short 5- minute break. This technique assists in focusing on the work requiring high concentration while at the same time having a chance to relax and avoid getting burnt out.
9. **Mindfulness and Meditation**: This is why people should practice mindfulness to enable them to develop an undistracted mind that is free from the influence of the digital world.

> **Random Fact:** A recent study found distinct brain changes in college students with high mobile phone addiction scores, including reduced grey matter volume in specific areas of the brain (BMC Psychiatry, 2023) (BioMed Central).

Long-term Benefits: Discussing the Positive Changes That Come with Reducing Digital Dependency

1. **Improved Mental Health**: This means that, in the long-term, reducing digital noise will help in the reduction of anxiety and stress levels, since notifications and other digital intrusions are known to cause these ailments.
2. **Enhanced Focus and Productivity**: Using the above example of less distraction being better for productivity, it can be seen that being away from a social network such as Facebook can help improve focus and therefore productivity.
3. **Better Sleep Quality**: Limiting the time spent in front of devices such as television, computer, tablet or smartphone and avoiding their use before bedtime results in improved sleep quality, which has a significant impact on the general well-being of an individual.
4. **Stronger Personal Relationships**: People are also able to have more time for family and friends since they do not spend most of their time on their digitally-linked devices.
5. **Greater Enjoyment of Real-Life Experiences**: With less time spent on digital devices, individuals often find more joy in real-life experiences, enhancing overall life satisfaction.

Now that you've got what you need, so to speak – the insights and strategies that will form the basis of your attack – the ball is in your court. Don't let technology take control of your life, instead make technology work for you and your lifestyle. Turn off those notifications, put your phone down and get a glimpse of the real world and remind yourself that your phone is just an instrument, not a source of survival.

It really is that simple.

Let's end this chapter on a positive note. We are not helpless, which means that it is possible to take back control of our digital realities. It will require some hard work and dedication, but I have complete and total faith in you!

> **Random Fact:** 55% of British smartphone users can't make it through dinner without looking at their phones (Exploding Topics, 2024) ([Exploding Topics](#)).

Action Plan:

1. **Conduct a Digital Audit:** Begin with evaluating how frequently you feel the phantom vibrations or the urge to glance at the mobile phone. Education is the key to the solution as people cannot be forced into change when they are unaware of the existence of a problem.
2. **Notification Cleanse:** Pick up your phone, and from the list of notifications, disable all of the ones

that aren't crucial. It can significantly decrease the frequency of being interrupted by your phone and losing focus from reality.

3. **Mindful Tech Usage:** One should agree on specific time for going through emails and social networks and not doing it intermittently during the day. This helps in regaining control over your time or attention span as it were.

4. **Digital Detox Rituals:** Using the electronic devices becomes a habit, so incorporating the no-phone hours or no-phone zones such as the dining table or not allowing the use of phones in the bedroom before going to bed will be helpful in relieving your mind off electronic stimuli.

CHAPTER 5

Likes, LOLs, and Loneliness: The Social Media Soup

Welcome to the digital masquerade ball where behind each username hides a character, status contains a drama, and each like an applause. This is the world of social media – the illusory world of interactions, where people are identified as friends in terms of followers and discussions are confined to comments only.

But if you look beyond this beautiful interface of dynamic online communication, there is a hidden truth. The irony is that the more connected we may appear, the sadder some of us may be. It is a scenario similar to being witnesses to the largest social gathering in the world and standing on the periphery.

So, let's start walking through this labyrinth of social media

– a realm that unites people of the entire planet but at the same time can alienate a person from the person sitting right beside him.

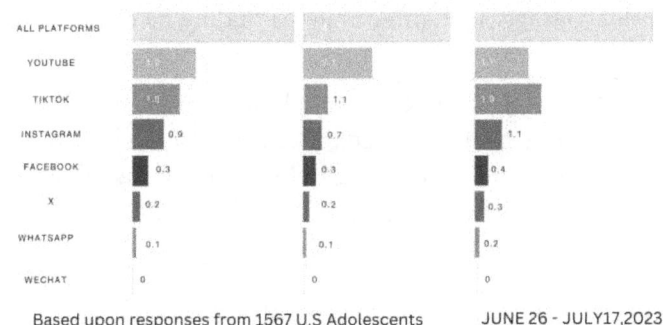

Source Gallup

The Digital Paradox: Connected But Alone

Among the sea of likes, shares, and an endless amount of scrolling , we have found a new mystery – the digital paradox. This basically translates to what some people refer to as the paradox of the modern society; we are more connected than ever before but at the same time, we are lonelier than we have ever been.

Definition and Exploration

As one of the pillars of the digital paradox, the nature of our online interactions is the most significant issue. In this world, we are connected more than ever but often feel isolated, like we are drowning in the ocean of connections and still are desperately lonely. We type messages, post pictures of what we ate for dinner last night, and write status updates, thus making people think that we have an active social life. However, these kinds of interactions are not as fulfilling, meaningful, or personal as being able to talk to someone in person. We are the performers who tread the board of a social media play, with invisible spectators and the encouragement, oftentimes, sounding fake.

> **Random Fact:** Almost half of Americans say they've been phubbed by their partner due to smartphone use (Exploding Topics, 2024) (Exploding Topics).

Expert Insights

Famous psychologists and sociologists have tried to explain this paradox, and as a result, the effects of virtual connection on actual relations have become clear. Sherry Turkle's TED statement "We're all connected but are we really alone?" is focused on new definitions of relationships and interactions given by technology and social media. According to Turkle, on one hand technology helps us to communicate with other people, but on the other hand, it isolates us as long as we do not communicate with people face to face and build true relationships.

Moreover, the American Psychological Association has also debated the relationship between technology and loneliness and how our dependence on technology to satisfy our need for acceptance and affection results in the fear of actual closeness. This constant connectivity alters some of the ways we may think of ourselves and the roles we play in social structures.

In one respect, the digital paradox is a choice that is self-evident but still fraught with a range of difficulties when implemented. In this context, it is vitally important to stay aware of what we are consuming online and try to contribute to the world in a positive manner through technology. It is now important to strive to have a healthy blend of online life with offline life so that the virtual world is not taken up all the real world.

> **Random Fact:** 71% of people spend more time on their phones than with their romantic partner (Exploding Topics, 2024) (Exploding Topics).

The Currency of Attention: Likes and Validation

This new social media market has transformed 'likes' into the new gold, 'shares' into silver and 'comments' into shining jewels. This is the new world of the market of attention, in which every individual is on both the demand and supply side. Thus, the question begs the answer, "what is the price of trading in this virtual money?"

Social Media Dynamics

The ever-evolving nature of social media platforms means that once positive symbols of 'being liked' has now become a way of measuring acceptability. Every one of the thumbs up is a sign of affirmation, a virtual high-five, which perpetuates the chase for the next. Likes and comments, on the other hand, are similar to the voices of the digital self, giving life to the existence in this vast world of the web. But as we run after these symbols of approval and affirmation on social media, are we losing fragments of ourselves?

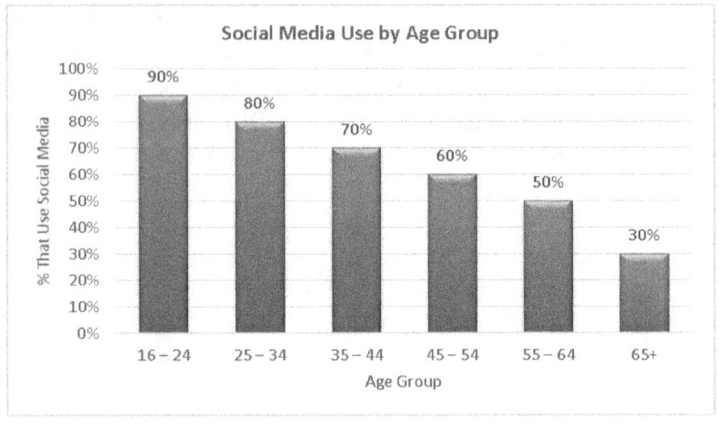

Psychological Analysis

What this new form of currency does to our heads and self-worth cannot be overstated. A spike of likes can be compared to the consumption of cocaine – a temporary kick that activates the pleasure part of our brain. However, what happens when the likes do not follow? The verification that all of us desire and oftentimes yearn for is elusive and fickle. It is like constructing our emotional house on the sand – the digital sand that is fragile and can change in an instant.

This constant search for acceptance can make social media exhausting as it turns into an attempt to constantly construct the best version of ourselves online, which can be far from who we really are. This is a lot of pressure to keep up what we can see as a facade for a never-ending show that has an audience constantly craving for more.

> **Random Fact:** Around 1 in 8 smartphone users have interrupted intimacy to check their phone (Exploding Topics, 2024) ([Exploding Topics](#)).

Case Studies

Take, for example, a teenage girl, Emily, who developed her self-esteem based on the number of followers and likes on her social media profiles. A post with fewer likes would make her feel that nobody likes her or that the world was a terrible place. Recently, a survey conducted by the Royal Society for Public Health in the UK reported that social media, especially Instagram, was linked with increased rate of anxiety and depression among the youth.

This example echos a common theme: the desire of being validated on the digital level can take us further on the path of suffering. They are a harsh wake-up call about social media – the construct that brings hope and an ability to bring people together, but at the same time is a pit that can swallow whole your self-esteem and health.

Strategies

1. **Authenticity Over Perfection**: To gain any form of connection with someone is to be real with their feelings. It's important to be yourself and not just present the most glamorous and perfect version of yourself.

2. **Engage Meaningfully**: Don't just scroll through the pages here and there. When commenting, it is necessary to provide a purpose, initiate a discussion, and contribute to the discussion. The friendships, relationships, and contacts are not created by the number of people one knows but by the nature of these associations.
3. **Join Interest-Based Communities**: The Internet is rich in communities formed based on common interest. Whether it is a book club on Facebook, a workout crew on Instagram, or a professional affiliation on LinkedIn, these groups can be a help and a source of real camaraderie.
4. **Social Media Sabbaticals**: Sometimes it is good to shut down your computer and get back online. Stepping away from social media sites is good in ensuring that one is not over stretched and that the whole experience is invigorating.

> Random Fact: 56% of children and adolescents use their smartphones after midnight at least three times per week (Exploding Topics, 2024) (Exploding Topics).

Positive Use

The positive effects of social media when used in moderation are to supplement rather than to replace real-life social contacts. This is a means of reconnection with friends who live in other parts of the country that are eager to find out what is happening in the neighborhood and initiating discussions that may lead to meeting up physically. Here's some strategies:

1. **Initiate Offline Meetups**: Engage in local meet up groups, reading clubs, clubs or any other group that is formed based on interests. It's an excellent opportunity that internet acquaintances can easily turn into actual life friendships.
2. **Leverage Platforms for Social Good**: Participate or start online trending for social issues. Not only does this promote that feeling of community but it also creates a real change that can be seen.
3. **Balance is Key**: What is more important to understand here is that the purpose is not to replace real-life conversations with text-based ones. As much as possible, seek to achieve moderation as social media is just among the many things that you engage in in life.

So, let our social media be a tool with which to open the doors, but let us not fail to step out into the big, beautiful world they lead to!

> **Random Fact:** 66.4% of children spend four hours or more per day on their smartphones (Exploding Topics, 2024) (Exploding Topics).

Action Plan:

1. **Embrace Authenticity:** It's safer to share your authentic personality on social media rather than projecting a false image. People are more likely to read and respond to genuine posts because the interactions are more meaningful.

2. **Engage Intentionally:** This is a call to action for brands and individuals to move beyond merely scrolling and liking posts. Instead, approach your posts thoughtfully, initiate discussions, and respond to comments in ways that foster open and meaningful communication.

3. **Find Your Tribe:** This means seeking out social media groups or forums centered around your hobbies and interests. These platforms should offer a social outlet and the opportunity to connect with like-minded individuals.

4. **Create Offline Connections:** Integrate social media interaction with the face-to-face interactions. Attend various meetings, communities, or sessions that you want to be part of or contribute to with your ideas.

CHAPTER 6

The Never-Ending Workday: Thanks, Smartphone!

There was a time, not so long ago, when the words "work" and "home" were as distinct as coffee and tea. These were the days when offices had walls, and 'remote' was just a way to describe a far-off, exotic vacation spot. Then along came a little gadget – the smartphone – and suddenly, these boundaries blurred faster than your vision after 2 drinks at the bar on Friday night.

The smartphone, initially hailed as a beacon of convenience, has stealthily morphed into an omnipresent force in our lives. It's like that friend who says they'll just crash on your couch for a night and ends up staying for a year. We welcomed it into our world to make calls, send texts, and maybe play the odd game of Wordle. But now, it's the boss who can reach you at midnight, the client who expects a reply on Sunday, and the constant pings that have replaced the peaceful chirps of morning birds.

The 24/7 Work Culture: How Smartphones Blur Work-Life Boundaries

In the pre-smartphone era, the end of the workday was marked by a simple, yet powerful ritual – shutting down your computer and leaving the office. It was a physical and psychological sign that the day was done. Fast forward to today, and this clear-cut boundary has become extremely fuzzy.

I have a dear friend who is a manager for a very large business, and if a text comes in at 2am from work, they respond. 8pm on Friday night and they ask how can I help? The weekends are no exception. The line has definitely been blurred between time "off" and time "on."

> **Random Fact:** Baby Boomers spend the least amount of time on their smartphones, averaging 3 hours and 38 minutes daily (Demand Sage, 2024).

The Uninvited Guest at Dinner

Imagine you're sitting down for dinner on Saturday night with someone who you've been wanting to go out with for a long time. You have butterflies just thinking about getting to know them and finding out what makes them tick. The first 15 minutes goes swimmingly as you both tell stories about when you were kids, and all the mutual friends you have in common.

The laughs are coming pretty easy, and you are thinking to yourself "maybe I'll get lucky tonight." The salad course comes and you grab your fork to take the first bite, and suddenly – buzz, buzz, buzz – your date reaches into their pocket to retrieve what can only be called the ultimate mood killer.

Your date gives you the obligatory *"I'm so sorry, I have to take this"* as they excuse themselves to continue the call in the hallway. Ten minutes later, they return with another apology, and the meal continues. Then, right in the middle of a great story about how they got their first puppy, they reach for their phone to reply to the 3 texts that have come in just since they sat back down. , your perfect dinner plans is ruined.

This is a common story...there doesn't seem to be any boundaries anymore, and what constitutes appropriate and inappropriate behavior has been redefined.

This could happen at any gathering. You might be at your family dinner, eating and laughing at the jokes and suddenly you hear a buzz, your other hand instinctively reaches for the smartphone. It's an email from your boss, marked 'urgent', of course. The peaceful family dinner now plays second fiddle to a work crisis that couldn't wait until morning. This scenario, absurd as it may sound, has become a common occurrence in households everywhere. It is now apparent that our smartphones have turned us into Pavlov's dogs with a ring, a vibration or a beep from the device instantly eliciting a response.

The "Always On" Syndrome

Always On syndrome is an outcome of the increased usage of smartphones in the modern world. It's the aspect of always having to be on standby, always waiting for updates, always being in work mode. It is barely possible to distinguish between working and leisure time, as they seem to intermingle without clear separation.

Well, here is a lighter but serious take on this subject. Let me paint a picture for you: an actual picture or, if you prefer a more artistic approach, a graph. On one axis, we have 'Time of Day', and on the other, 'Work-Related Smartphone Use'. You might expect to see a steep decline after 5pm, resembling the drop of a rollercoaster. But it looks more like the heart rate monitor of someone watching a suspense thriller – constant spikes at all hours. From replying to emails at a child's birthday party to taking work calls on a Sunday morning, our smartphones ensure that work is always just a swipe away.

Redefining Workplace Expectations

Smartphones haven't just changed our habits; they've rewritten the rules of workplace engagement. It's like suddenly finding out that the game of Monopoly you've been playing all your life now includes a rule where you can buy properties via text.

Employers and clients now operate under the assumption that since you *can* be reached at any time, you *should* be available at all times. This 'on-demand' work culture has raised the bar for what's considered normal responsiveness, turning what used to be an after-hours emergency into just another Tuesday night.

> **Random Fact:** 95% of adults under 50 years use smartphones, compared to only 61% of those above 65 years (Demand Sage, 2024).

The Smartphone: Your New Office in Your Pocket

Today, your office is wherever your smartphone is —let's face it, that's practically everywhere. Whether it's the pocket of your gym shorts or the nightstand next to your bed, work is always just an arm's length away. It's like having a tiny boss that follows you around, whispering, "Just one more email," as you try to drift off to sleep.

Our new-found habits of always making ourselves available for work purposes doesn't stop at the office door. It also includes making ourselves available for friends and family 24/7. If our phone buzzes, we reach for it. If a call comes in, we feel obligated to answer it. Even if we are in the middle of doing something else! The boundaries have vanished into thin air, and we are now held captive by our device.

The Double-Edged Sword of Convenience

Sure, smartphones have made our lives more convenient. Need to send a quick email while on the go? Done. Want to edit a document from the comfort of your couch? Easy. But with great convenience comes great responsibility – or rather, the expectation of constant availability. It's a bit like being given a fancy sports car that can go zero to sixty in three seconds, only to find out you're expected to be on call for impromptu races at all hours. It may be exciting at first, but it eventually becomes exhausting.

The New Norm: Work-Life Blend

I've included a couple of BONUS chapters at the end of the book, one of them is about Lifestyle Design, and I firmly believe that if taken seriously, could change the direction of your life in a very positive way.

We used to talk about work-life balance, but let's be real – for many of us, it's more of a blend now, with work and personal life mixed together like a smoothie; that's half business, half pleasure. The problem is, when you're sipping on this work-life smoothie all day, it's tough to tell where the work ends and your real life begins. This new norm isn't necessarily bad, but it's essential to recognize how it's reshaping our daily lives and our well-being.

Digital Burnout: Recognizing the Signs

Ah, digital burnout – the modern age's badge of 'honor.' It's like being part of a club where the membership fee is your peace of mind, and the only perk is the ability to twitch at the sound of an email notification. But how do you know if you're a member of this not-so-exclusive club? Let's dive into the symptoms:

> **Random Fact:** 50% of kids in the United States aged 13 to 18 said that they are addicted to smartphones (Dove Recovery, 2023) (ATC Columbus).

The List of Symptoms

1. **The Phantom Vibration Syndrome**: You feel your phone vibrate, you reach for it with lightning speed just to realize it's just your imagination. This is the first sign that your mind and pocket have become a bit too cozy with each other.
2. **The 2AM Email Check**: If you find yourself waking up in the middle of the night and the first thing you do is check your email, congratulations! You're on the express train to Burnoutville.
3. **The Social Media Scroller's Thumb**: It's like the runner's knee for the digital age. If scrolling through your feeds is starting to feel like an Olympic sport, it's time to pause and reflect.
4. **The 'Just One More Email' Lie**: When you tell yourself, "I'll just reply to one more email," and

suddenly it's three hours later – welcome to the club.

> **Random Fact:** A recent study found distinct brain changes in college students with high mobile phone addiction scores, including reduced grey matter volume in specific areas of the brain (BMC Psychiatry, 2023) ([BioMed Central](#)).

Personal Anecdotes: The Human Side of the Story

Let me tell you about a friend, assuming he's 'Dave.' Dave used to be the life of the party, always ready with a joke or a funny story. But then, he got a smartphone for work. Slowly, the Dave we knew started to fade away, replaced by a man who was always typing, scrolling, and frankly, looking pretty stressed out. Last time I checked, Dave's idea of a wild Friday night was reorganizing his email folders. It's funny, yet kind of not.

Expert Insights: What the Pros Say

Science has been revealing the signs of digital burnout in people with increased frequency. In one study, people reported that connectivity can cause lower performance, dissatisfaction at the workplace, and increased rates of mental disorders. It is as if putting the wrong fuel in a car; at one point, the car will start to conk out.

The Mental Health Angle

It may be funny to make a joke at the expense of social interaction, but it is a serious concern when it comes to our mental health. Today's world is full of anxiety, depression, and sleeplessness, and with our constant connectivity, it only grows worse. Some days I feel like our brains are racing in a marathon, and there is no set path to the end line.

> **Random Fact:** Nearly 34% of users have problematic internet use habits, a trend that has grown because of the COVID-19 pandemic (SlickText, 2023).

Tethered to Work: More Than Just a Metaphor

The reality of being plugged in 24/7 through your smartphone is not just practical; it is a psychological drama. It is similar to being on a leash with the other end held by a boss who works twenty-four seven. This constant connection where your work life has infiltrated your living room, kitchen, and even your bedroom can create a feeling of entrapment.

The Rise of Workplace Digital Anxiety

Let me introduce you to the new form of fearing technology in the workplace – 'workplace digital anxiety.' It's the anxiety that emerges when you receive a notification of a new message in the workplace's email after working hours. That emotion experienced on Sundays before the beginning of the working week, before the heavy load of work online. This type of anxiety is not only about the company workload but because the company is invading the personal space. Can you picture yourself having a work shadow tagging along with you even on your spare time – not the most ideal buddy, I suppose?

Sidebar: Quick Facts and Stats

- **Did You Know?** A study showed that users who actively use their work email during off-working time, also experience higher levels of stress and anxiety.
- **Psychological Impact**: Constant smartphone use for work has been linked to increased risks of insomnia, anxiety, and depression.
- **The Numbers Speak**: A survey reveals that 60 percent of employees feel compelled to be always on due to smartphones, laptops, and other devices.

The Invisible Chains of Digital Connectivity

The social cost of living in a world that is so interconnected through the use of technology and the internet is extensive. It is like being shackled and these shackles are invisible, but they confine you to your work even when you are not aware of it. The result? A constantly running calendar that continues to function even when the owner of the mind needs a break. This can cause such symptoms as anxiety, to burn-out.

Breaking the Cycle

The way to escape it is not only to get physically away from your mobile phone; it is to get your head away from it. It's about establishing a psychological barrier between the home front and the working environment, which is often difficult.

This could mean that there are certain hours you are not allowed to use the phone, or there are certain sections of the house that are off-limits during working hours. It is all about conditioning the mind to think in a different way and to know that even though the employer may call at any time of the day or night, does not mean you have to answer.

We all need to have our own 'Montana' to escape to.

> **Random Fact:** 79% of Millennials put their phones right by them when they sleep, and 53% wake up at least once every night to check them (Techjury, 2023).

The Bigger Picture

In the overall perspective, it is not only a matter of improving your quality of life and alleviating the sufferings of workers experiencing workplace digital anxiety; it is also about constructing a better work culture for the future. A culture that respects personal space, acknowledges the need for psychological safety, and an understanding that the need to be constantly connected does not necessarily equate to efficiency. It is about shifting the focus from more to better: from 'How much can we achieve?' to 'How can we achieve it better?'

CHAPTER 7

Appy Ever After? The Myth of Productivity Apps

It was just an ordinary Tuesday – or so I thought - when the computer screen flashed an unexpected message across the room. On that day, I woke up with a revelation. But unlike Archimedes, I didn't run through the streets shouting "Eureka!" Instead, I stared at my phone and mumbled, "Seriously, Mitche?"

There it was, in all its digital glory: Despite having an excel list full of these applications, my productivity had lowered significantly. There were apps that grouped other apps, reminders that were for the purpose of reminding me of other reminders, and trackers that tracked how much I was tracking. It was like bringing in a clown to juggle your juggling balls as you are still practicing them for the first time.

This is the land of digital clichés where the dream of productivity apps falls between the receptionist and the reality. Fasten your seat belts and let's wade through the seemingly endless sea of apps and widgets to find out which ones are angels, and which are demons that will waste your time.

The Overload of Digital Tools: When Productivity Becomes Counterproductive

Imagine this: you are in a restaurant, your eyes shining with temptation of a delicious banquet awaiting you. But instead of food, they take socially necessary time to use the productivity apps. They're spread out on your plate – a task manager here, a habit tracker there, and a new calendar app over there! You wake up one morning and your plate has been filled with so much that you hit the turkey status before you know it.

Welcome to the paradox of productivity apps. It's a bit like having a Swiss Army knife with a thousand tools; sure, it can do everything, but good luck finding the bottle opener when you need it. The more apps you download, the less productive you become. It's like trying to run a marathon while wearing every pair of shoes you own – just because you can, doesn't mean you should.

Let's talk about 'app overload.' This is the digital equivalent of hoarding. You download an app for every task, hoping to streamline your life. But instead of a well-oiled machine, you end up with a clunky, digital Frankenstein that's more confusing than your grandma using a smartphone for the first time.

I remember an old friend of mine that had an app for everything – even an app to remind him to drink water. True story.

Are we so glued to our screens that we've forgotten basic human functions? He was so tangled in his web of apps; he had forgotten what he was trying to organize in the first place.

Then, there's the tale of Sarah. She had so many productivity apps, she needed a spreadsheet to keep track of them all. Sarah's work schedule every day involved constant switching between apps, updating tasks on the go, and synchronizing calendars. Instead of gaining time, she lost hours to the very instruments that were meant to cut the time she devoted to typing. This had turned into a never-ending cycle of trying to achieve the best productivity and had become counterproductive.

They can cause what is known as decision fatigue. This is a situation where you are overwhelmed with choices in an environment that is filled with screens. It's a huge burden to require attention, decisions, and time – and let's face it, we have better things to do like remember to wear pants in the morning.

As we wander through this electronic forest, do not forget that it's not the number of tools, but the value of the tools and the way in which they are employed that counts. How you exercise in the gym is very important, because you could have a membership card all your life and not get fit at all. To the same extent, possessing a multitude of apps is not equal to efficiency; it is how you employ these apps that defines efficiency.

So, as we continue this journey, let's ask ourselves: Are we lords of our smartphones or are we just clusters of apps that do not seem necessary at all?

> **Random Fact:** 69% of teens wish they could spend more time face-to-face with their close friends, but 52% of them simply sit together without talking, or using their cell phones for long periods (Screen Education, 2023) ([Enterprise Apps Today](#)).

Evaluating Productivity Apps: The Art of Selective Downloading

First of all, let me give you an example of the battle plan that we need to adopt. App selection for the productivity enhancement is not just a casual affair like having many one-night stands but rather it is more of finding a soul mate application.

Ask yourself: Does this app effectively address a certain need or enhance an activity? Is this a first date, arranged by the app, the real thing, or is it the same as the ghosting phenomenon that occurred with the latest popular application last week?

Search for the apps that would serve your personal and professional life, and those that will not simply flutter in and out of your life like a butterfly, but rather will be as constant as your loyal black lab.

> **Random Fact:** The average teenager sends approximately 3,300 SMS messages every month (Enterprise Apps Today, 2023).

Decluttering Your Digital Space

In this section, let us gear up for the next step that is the actual process of decluttering. Start with the app audit. Check every app and ask:

1. **When was the last time I used this?** If it's been collecting digital dust for months, it's time to say goodbye.
2. **Does this app duplicate functions of another app I have?** If you've got overlapping apps, choose the best and ditch the rest.
3. **Does this app genuinely enhance my productivity?** If it's just a 'nice to have' and not a 'need to have,' it's probably not essential.

Remember, each app should have a clear purpose and a distinct role in your productivity playbook. It's like a sports team – you want the best players in their positions, working seamlessly together to score goals, not tripping over each other on the field.

In this digital detox, you might feel a twinge of FOMO as you part with certain apps. But trust me, the peace of digital simplicity is worth it. Soon, you'll find that with fewer, but more effective tools, your productivity soars like an eagle, unburdened by the unnecessary weight of redundant apps.

> **Random Fact:** 91.8% of people use and/or look at their phones while watching TV (Reviews.org, 2023).

Mindful Usage: Balancing Digital Convenience with Real Productivity

Now that we've pruned the digital garden, it's time to cultivate mindful app usage. It is like having a powerful car with great features such as a high acceleration rate but you do not know how to drive it without causing an accident.

The Zen of App Usage

It is the act of deliberately using your smart gadget by choice and not as a result of the routine or habit. It's the difference between picking up your phone consciously, with a specific goal in mind, and listlessly flicking through your apps like the walking dead, desperate for your next fix of digital brain-food.

Setting Boundaries: The Digital Fence

To avoid being trapped in the rat race of 'busy work,' be sure to establish healthy expectations with your productivity tools. You should allocate time for purposes such as checking e-mails, revisiting the to-do list, or developing your time schedule.

That is like having a schedule for when to use the tools in

your office for work. These are some ways in which you can ensure that your apps are resting when they are not in use, apart from these hours. In this manner, you structure your day, and you are not subjected to the whims of the various gadgets that surround you.

Just as a reminder, productivity is not the time where your applications are launched, but it's the time which is managed wisely. It is all about the right things being done and not people doing things rightly.

Case Study: The Digital Minimalist

Here is Alex, a man who used to be an app addict and who became a digital minimalist in a blink of an eye. It was like being at a wild party where every app is trying to lure you to pay attention to it. Notifications came like bees in a hive and with each sting, he lost a part of himself.

First, Alex overhauled the entire app list, removing all the nonessential applications and leaving only the most useful ones. Subsequently, Alex set rigid practices that prohibited working after 6 pm and limited time on social media to lunch breaks. The first few days were difficult, as are the first few days without caffeine for the digital soul, but the effect was mind-boggling.

Alex's productivity skyrocketed, and he had plenty of time to work and concentrate on complex thinking and problem solving. Whereas previously, it would take days to accomplish some projects, but now it was possible to do them in a couple of hours. Alex was able to find those hobbies that were abandoned over the years such as painting and hiking, which used to take that amount of time in front of computer devices. Alex even began to read actual books again, not those ones where the pages are screens, you know, the paper ones?

Let me ask this questions again...what would you do with an extra 1 hour every day to do with whatever you wanted?

The change was so complete that people in his community started telling stories of how Alex became someone else. To learn more about it, friends and colleagues who witnessed this miraculous transformation began to turn to experts. Alex started to give out suggestions on how to adopt digital minimalism and later offered a series of lessons on how to use applications mindfully. From this use of technology and its intentionality, it was clearly a ripple effect of positivity.

Remember this: your phone is an instrument, not a master. If used properly it does not take over your life, but you use it in such a way that it becomes useful and helpful. Take a cue from what you've just read and learn how to make the most of the digital tools you have but use them less, and more effectively.

It's not just about creating more space on your device – you get to create more space in your life for everything that matters.

We have seen that being busy is now a status symbol especially in the modern society where everyone is rushing to get something done, but the question that we should be asking ourselves is not how busy we are, but how effective we are. It is all about how we can use our time efficiently and how we can efficiently use the tools at our disposal.

So, the next time you reach for your phone, pause and ask yourself: "Is this intentional, or is it just a habit?" Your answer might just be the key to unlocking a more productive, balanced, and fulfilling life.

> **Random Fact:** 45% of users admit texting at least once while driving (Techjury, 2023).

Action Plan:

1. **Embrace Digital Minimalism:** Quality over quantity should be the order of the day when it comes to apps. Eliminate the ones that add no value to your activities and are not essential for your health.

2. **Intentional App Interaction:** Just as a reminder, when using this app or any other similar app, one should ask himself whether he needs it or it's simply a routine for him. Focus on being intentional when using apps and use them only for their intended function.

3. **Explore Alternatives to Digital Tools:** It is advised that one should try to incorporate non-digital tools for planning and organizing tasks like the conventional paper calendar.

CHAPTER 8

The 7-Day Digital Detox Plan

In today's world where our gadgets are firmly fixed in our palms like a koala to a tree, sometimes it is possible to lose sight of the fact that there is a big more extensive world out there. The 'Groundhog Day' moment that we all live now, is playing out in front of the screen instead of the small creature.

But what if we stopped this digital world for a while and analyzed it? What if we decided to take a step back and unlearn the art of 'app'iness for life thereafter? This is where our digital detoxification process starts. It's not about burying your devices into the sea, or even for a moment desiring to do so, but about learning the balance between the ping of a notification and the stillness of no noise at all.

> **Random Fact:** 31% of parents say screen usage is the third most common cause of disagreement between parents and teenagers (Techjury, 2023).

Day 1

Morning Ritual: The Unplugged Awakening

Morning Zen Zone

Scene Setting: Give yourself 30 minutes in the morning to wake up and have a peaceful start to the day. This could be burning the candle that gives the scent of fresh forest after a rainfall or simply switching on the window to allow the morning light to come in. Grab a cup of coffee and start your day without your device. You can create a space that screams (or rather, whispers), "tranquility."

Digital Devices: Now, this is crucial - no phones, tablets, or gadgets that go beep in the morning. They're like that one friend who talks too much – not needed in our Zen Zone.

Mindfulness Maneuvers

Activity Options: Engage in a mindfulness activity. This could be meditation – and no, you don't need to be a Zen master for this. Simple deep breathing exercises, a gentle yoga flow, or stretching like you're reaching for the last cookie on the top shelf works too.

Presence Over Pixels: The idea here is to be completely in the moment. If your mind wanders to your digital devices, gently bring it back. It's like training a puppy – patience and persistence.

> **Random Fact:** More than half of teenagers think they use their smartphones for too long (Enterprise Apps Today, 2023).

Digital Reality Check

Typical Morning vs. Today: Think about your normal morning routine. How often is your phone the first thing you reach for, even before a coffee? Today, observe how this tranquil start contrasts with your usual, device-dominated dawn.

Digital Audit: Tracking Your Digital Footprint

The Device Diary

Keeping Track: Each time you feel the urge to check a device, write it down. Note the time, how long you used it, and why. Was it necessary or just a habit?

Honesty is Key: Remember, this is a no-judgment zone. You're not trying to win an award for Least Phone Checks. It's about understanding your digital habits.

Setting Intentions: The Digital Detox Plan

Goal Setting: Write down specific digital detox goals. It could be something like, "I will only check my email at 10 AM and 4 PM" or "My phone will not join me at meal times." These are your digital boundaries – set them like you mean it.

Affirmation Time: Create a personal affirmation related to your detox goal. Something like, "I am more than my screen time" or "I engage with the world, not just my device." Repeat this throughout the day, like a catchy tune you can't get out of your head.

> **Random Fact:** 89% of parents blame themselves and caregivers for their children's cell phone addiction (Techjury, 2023).

Day 2

The Digital Declutter - "The Great Unsubscribe and App Amputation"

Morning: The Great Unsubscribe

1. **Email Exorcism**
    - **Inbox Inventory**: Dive into your email. Start unsubscribing from newsletters, promos, and updates that don't spark joy. Think of it as decluttering your digital closet.
    - **Ruthless Review**: Ask yourself, "Does this email feed my curiosity or just clog my day?" If it's the latter, hit unsubscribe. Remember, every unneeded email is like a mosquito at a barbecue – annoying and unnecessary.

2. **Example for Clarity**: Imagine you're subscribed to 'Larry's Llama Facts'. Sure, llamas are cool, but if you're not planning to start a llama farm, maybe it's time to say goodbye to Larry.

Afternoon: App Amputation

1. **App Audit**
   - **Screen Scrutiny**: Scroll through your phone or computer. Look at each app and ask, "Do I really need this, or is it just a digital dust collector?"
   - **Harsh Reality**: If an app is more about habit than help, or if it tends to send you down a rabbit hole of negativity, it's time for it to go.
2. **Example for Perspective**: Let's say you have an app, 'Frenzy of Fish' - a game where you build an aquarium. It's fun, but if you're spending more time with virtual fish than real people, it might be time for 'Frenzy of Fish' to sleep with the fishes.

Evening: Tech-Free Family Time

1. **Family Fun-teraction**
   - **Plan an Activity**: Choose something that fosters interaction. Could be a board game that brings out the competitive spirit, a

puzzle that tests your collective patience, or a DIY art project that ends in laughter and glitter everywhere.
- **Engagement Over Electronics**: Use this time to really connect. Talk about your day, share stories, or discuss the digital detox journey.

Reflect and Share

- **Digital Detox Discussion**: In the final moments of the game or activity, facilitate a discussion regarding the participants' experiences during any tech-less period. What did the participants think about it? Did they miss their devices? Were the participants more active during the activity?
- **Insight Exchange**: Tell me your thoughts about what you've done in the context of digital decluttering today. Explain what emotions one can possibly experience when using the 'unsubscribe' button or deleting an application. Was it liberating? Challenging?

> **Random Fact:** 72% of teens feel that people expect them to respond immediately to notifications (Techjury, 2023).

Day 3

Self-Discovery through Solitude

1. **Solo Time**
   - **Activity Selection**: Select an event to attend that can help you reflect on your life and enjoy yourself at the same time. Maybe it is reading a book that you have been interested in or writing your diary, tending to the plants, or even cooking a new dish.
   - **Digital Distraction-Free**: Make sure there are no digital distractions in this activity, to the students or the instructor. For instance, think that your phone is left somewhere on a beach on an isolated island with no network signals.
2. **Inner Reflection**
   - **Reflective Writing**: It may be useful to write in a journal during this period to record your reflections or feelings. You can also imagine how you feel when you are

unable to go through your emails or any of the other social networks. What is your growing awareness of yourself as a person?
- **Emotional Check-In**: Also, consider reflecting on your emotions. Are you apprehensive, less nervous, and set free? It is like doing a system check but with the aspect of the emotions that one have to face in a certain period.

For example, let's say you want to paint a picture. While blending paints and moving the brush to the canvas, you are not just painting but are pouring out feelings that are buried under the daily scroll of notifications. It is cathartic, bringing out aspects in you that you might not have thought of acknowledging.

> **Random Fact:** 41% of teens feel overwhelmed by the number of notifications they receive daily (Techjury, 2023) (Techjury).

Day 4

Nature Therapy

1. **Green Getaway**
    - **Plan an Outdoor Activity**: It could be a short nature trail, a walk in the park, or a

visit to your backyard in the evening. The idea is to engage the body with the surrounding environment or to become one with the nature.
- **Sensory Engagement**: Narrow your attention to the things that are present in the environment around you. Take a moment to look at the veins of the foliage, the traces of the cumulonimbus, the song of the sparrows. It is a registry of natural beauty, a phenomenon that goes unnoticed in a world dominated by social media and personal computers.

2. **Mindful Connections**
   - **Conversation Commitment**: Talk, if possible, in a conversation that is meaningful as well as face-to-face. This could be with a friend, a family member or even a neighbor who you are comfortable to be around with.
   - **Active Listening**: This means that you should listen carefully to what is being said by the other person, and nothing else should distract you. It's about attentiveness in the most literal sense, meaning being in the moment, not just in body, but in mind as well.

Example of Nature Therapy:

Imagine, you are strolling in a park and decide to stand still and observe a squirrel. It is ordinary, but it is a glimpse into humanity's interaction with nature that is real and unadulterated. One day, you decide to share your thoughts on what the squirrel was doing; you find yourself having a hearty laugh with yourself, and a good laugh with the stranger.

> **Random Fact:** Smartphone addiction has been linked to sleep disturbances, tech-no-stress, low self-confidence, social isolation, and depression among adolescents (Frontiers in Psychiatry, 2023) ([BioMed Central](#)).

Day 5

New Hobby Exploration

1. **Hobby Selection**
    - **Choose Your Adventure**: This is your chance to go for something new and get that experience which you have never had before. Perhaps, there is a pastime which you have always wanted to try but never had the chance to, say painting, baking, carpentry, or playing a guitar.

- **Embrace the Beginner's Mindset**: Just bear in mind that it is not about being perfect in every single thing that you do in the preparation for the examination. It is more about wandering and having fun. You could drop the ball and that is fine because it is one of the many ways in which people play the game.

2. **Dedicated Time**
   - **Immerse Yourself**: Spare a few hours for this newfound interest. Notice how engaging in a new activity can shift your focus from the digital world to the tangible, creative process in front of you.

Example of Hobby Exploration:

Let's say you choose baking. You start with a simple recipe, perhaps your world-famous chocolate chip cookies. As you measure the flour, crack the eggs, and mix the dough, you're not just creating a treat; you're crafting an experience.

Baking has a certain flow to it, a certain music, and I think that is why it is best described as a dance. And the smell – it is rather like a wonderful, sweet tinkle for the olfactory nerves. In addition, there is nothing quite as satisfying as savoring the food prepared by you. Priceless.

> **Random Fact:** Smartphone addiction can lead to reduced libido and sexual function, harming sexual relationships (Open Access Government, 2023).

Day 6

Community Engagement

1. **Finding Community Activities**
    - **Local Exploration**: Make an effort to find ways to engage your community. It can be focused on a volunteer activity, participating in a community garden, or visiting a local event.
    - **Social Impact**: This means to be a constructive member of society; do things that have a positive effect on your environment. This is about doing something which can change somebody's life or the community in which one resides in, take it a step at a time.
2. **Reflecting on the Experience**
    - **Sense of Belonging**: Following these interactions, consider the differences between these forms of communication and

digital ones. Pixels may hold the power to imitate reality, but there is a depth in context that they cannot capture.
- **Community Connection**: Think about the new relationships and networks you're building. These are your 'real-life social networks' – no Wi-Fi required.

Example of Community Engagement:

You decide to participate in a local park clean-up. As you pick up litter, you strike up conversations with fellow volunteers. You find out one of them shares your newfound interest in baking, while another offers gardening tips. These interactions, filled with laughter and learning, enrich your sense of community. It's a stark contrast to the often-impersonal nature of digital communication.

Day 7

Reflection and Forward Planning - "Assessing the Journey and Embracing the Future"

Assessing the Journey

1. **Quiet Reflection**
    - **Find a Peaceful Spot**: Choose a serene place where you can sit undisturbed. This might be your favorite armchair, a spot in your garden, or even a local park.

- **Journey Review**: Reflect on the past week. Think about the high points and the challenges. How did you feel during the various activities? What surprised you about your digital detox experience?
2. **Tech Relationship Reassessment**
    - **Digital Dependency**: Consider how your relationship with technology has changed. Do you find yourself reaching for your phone less? Are you more mindful of the time you spend on digital devices?
    - **Emotional and Mental Shifts**: Acknowledge any changes in your mental and emotional state. Are you feeling more present, less stressed, or more connected to the people and world around you?

> **Random Fact:** 78% of teens check their devices at least once an hour (Techjury, 2023).

Example of Reflection:

Imagine sitting with a cup of tea, looking back over the week. You recall the initial discomfort of not checking your phone first thing in the morning, the joy of baking those cookies, the laughter during the board game night, and the sense of community at the park clean-up. It's like watching a movie of your week, noticing how the scenes of life are richer and more colorful without the constant digital interruption.

Planning Ahead

1. **Realistic Digital Usage Plan**
    - **Set Practical Guidelines**: Considering your current schedule, develop a strategy for how you are going to use digital media during the upcoming week. This may entail setting certain hours in the day for reading and responding to e-mail, prohibiting the use of electronics in certain areas of the house, or having days of the week when no technology is allowed.
    - **Balance is Key**: Just the same, you have to remember that it is your experience, and you have to make sure that the balance that you are making is the one that is suitable for you. Technology is one thing, and it is not a leash that keeps individuals from pursuing their dreams.
2. **Incorporating Positive Habits**
    - **Daily Routine Integration**: Consider what you can do to integrate them into your everyday life so that you continue to

practice the new positive habits. Perhaps, it may be waking up with a morning meditation or ensuring that the family refrain from using electronic devices for some hours in a day.

- o **Long-Term Goals**: There are several tips that can be given towards the achievement of these goals as follows; maybe there are other hobbies you'd like to try out or perhaps you'd like to be more active in your community. List these down and try to think on how they could be attained in the most possible way.

Example of Planning Ahead:

Instead of mindlessly checking your phone the first thing when waking up, you begin the day with a 10-minute meditation. You also keep at least two days of the week as technology-free days for you to spend quality time with your family or get engrossed in a passion. As for the long-term goals, you would like to contribute your monthly volunteer work in activities within the community, establishing 'real-world' relationships.

Maintaining Balance: Strategies for Long-Term Digital Wellbeing

In the aftermath of our digital detox journey, the real challenge begins: maintaining this newfound equilibrium in our daily lives. The detox is not just a fleeting retreat; it's a springboard into a lifestyle where we coexist harmoniously with technology, not at its mercy.

> **Random Fact:** 57% of parents try to restrict their teen's use of social media (Enterprise Apps Today, 2023).

Setting Healthy Boundaries with Technology

The first aspect of this long-term partnership is to establish boundaries in a sound manner. This means having to take some time and important aspects of our lives and make them 'technologically' free. Think about your bedroom, dining room or living room that turns into a sacred space that is free from digital interactions. Here, people speak, read, and rest – all the while, screens do not disrupt the peace.

But, there should be 'no tech time'; such as during a meal, the first waking hour in the morning, or before going to bed. These periods are not about what we're missing online, but about what we're gaining in the real world: Having presence, feeling connected, and finding a way to calm oneself.

And that is why consuming media content with more attention is crucial. As we scroll through the social media, or news feeds- as it often happens, you should ask, "Do I really need this?" and that little check brings about some kind of awareness to the life we lead online.

Mindful Engagement with Digital Devices

Even this process should be conducted mindfully, with full awareness of what we are doing to ourselves and the world around us. Every time we grab our phone or switch on our laptop, it is important to reflect the purpose behind this action.

Simplifying the way we interact digitally can break us free from patterns that may not be productive, and guide us towards more meaningful ones. It's time to replace the idly scrolling with something more productive – calling a friend, reading an article on one's favorite hobby, or listening to a podcast that teaches something new and interesting.

It's crucial to introduce mindfulness protocols in our technical activities to change the approach to using devices. For example, it is possible to close the tab with the email or a social media account that just opened, and then, for ten seconds, just breathe in and breathe out deeply. It grounds us and puts us in a position where we are ready to face the digital realm in a more intentional way. It is suggested that the reflective practice of our media literacy should be conducted on a weekly basis, allowing us to be aware of our habits and change our behavior accordingly.

> **Random Fact:** Only 17% of Americans would go into debt to purchase a cell phone, a decrease from previous years (Reviews.org, 2023).

Integrating Offline Moments into Everyday Life

Real life presents itself with numerous possibilities about how 'unplugged' routines may be integrated. These rituals may be a morning walk, writing a diary or engaging in a form of art, and they act as markers, helping us remain in our physical reality. They enable us to embrace the natural simplicity in life that technology so often conceals. These points are important as it keeps practicing the habits that are developed during the digital detox until they become habits to be followed always.

To maintain the good vibes of detoxification, set a tone to check for occasional tech breaks. Whether it is one day per week or one weekend per month, these times are important opportunities to pause, reassess our online behaviors and reconnect with whatever we enjoy in real life. They make us recall the joy of life, which is not limited to the time spent in front of screens, thus they emphasize the work on the balance we pursue.

Fostering a Balanced Family Environment

A balanced digital life is not just an individual quest; it is our family and certainly our community. Discussions that involve the whole family in sharing and establishing rules towards the use of digital devices go a long way in developing a culture towards the technology. Screen-free family activities mean that children, as well as the entire family, benefit from healthier relationships that encourage face-to-face interaction rather than turning to screens.

By being proactive and setting our own positive example, others will be encouraged to adopt a healthy approach towards the use of digital devices. In my opinion, this is the best way to show everyone the advantages of maintaining this kind of equilibrium by our own example. It is useful to motivate the family members or flat mates to spend time on offline activities like playing games, going outside, or working on a project together so that everyone is aware of the need to take a break from technology.

The process of achieving and maintaining the balanced use of technology in our daily lives is a continuous and evolving process. It is about learning what is good for the individual and the people one is interacting with, and also being open to change as the situation shifts. It is always inspiring to encourage a family or a group of people to go for small achievements that will make them happy in the long run. Maybe it is an evening not spent glued to television or endlessly chatting on phones, but one filled with humor and discussions or a weekend where the devices and technology step aside in favor of outdoor and discovery. These are some of the simplest moments that can collectively create a shift towards living a life that is more conscious, engaged, and meaningful.

It is important to recall that our screens are merely devices, not our rulers in this postmodern society with technology domination. This is not a case of escaping from the digital realm altogether; it's about being able to live within it in a way that enhances our lives and at the same time embracing and appreciating those precious real life moments which might not make it to the small screen.

In concluding this chapter, it can be seen that the transition through the digital detox and the subsequent process of recovery to a more balanced digital lifestyle is much more than just a temporary break from the oppressive embrace of technology. It is quite transformative to the outlook of life as more than a screen experience. Thus, we have explored the difficult but worthwhile process of completing the 7-Day Digital Detox Plan, rekindled our love for offline activities, and learned the ways to endure and come out victorious.

> **Random Fact:** Smartphone addiction can lead to tolerance, where more internet use is needed to get the same degree of satisfaction (Open Access Government, 2023).

Action Plan:

1. **Regular Offline Activities:** To counteract the negativity of such interactions, engage in activities like reading, gardening, or taking a walk to bring you back to reality.

2. **Family and Community Engagement:** Reduce screen time for yourself and your family and engage in real life activities both within a family environment and the wider community.

3. **Ongoing Mindfulness:** Take a break and do some deep breathing and meditation to be present with your online behaviours and any effects they have on you.

CHAPTER 9

Screen Time to Scream Time: The Fatal Cost of Mobile Multitasking

These miracles of modern technology that we have in our pocket, which have made the world connected, can make us more disconnected from the roads, from the environment, and from our own judgment.

Imagine this: you're cruising at 55 mph, eyes glued to your phone, texting away. Guess what? You've just driven the length of a football field blindfolded. Congratulations, you're now a magician of sorts, but the kind nobody wants to share the road with.

Why Texting Behind the Wheel is Like Juggling Chainsaws

When you text and drive, you're not just multitasking; you're tri-tasking! Visually, manually, and cognitively distracted – it's like trying to juggle chainsaws while balancing on a unicycle. You're looking at your phone, typing a message, and mentally crafting that perfect emoji response, all while neglecting the two-ton metal beast you're commanding. Spoiler alert: it's not going to end well.

The Dangers: More Than Just Typos

The risks of texting and driving are as clear as the 'Do Not Enter' sign you just missed. It's a cocktail of danger – with a twist of insanity. According to our friends at the NHTSA, distracted driving, spearheaded by texting, is a chart-topper for causing vehicle crashes in the U.S. It's like playing Russian roulette with your car, but the bullets are text messages.

Confessions of a Distracted Driver

AAA found out that while 96% of drivers think texting and emailing while driving is a serious threat, 39% admitted to reading texts behind the wheel. It's like acknowledging that fire is hot but still playing with matches. And the cherry on top? Texting while driving can impair your reaction time as much as downing four beers in an hour. Who needs a bar when you've got a smartphone, right?

> **Random Fact:** India is home to the world's largest "unconnected" population, with 730 million people not using the internet at the start of 2023 (DataReportal – Global Digital Insights, 2023).

The Hangover Effect

After texting, it takes your brain about 27 seconds to reorient to the road. It's called the hangover effect, and it doesn't come with any of the fun stories from the night before. Just potential car crashes.

> **Random Fact:** Students who did not use their phones during a lecture wrote down 62% more information and scored a grade and a half higher on a test (Enterprise Apps Today, 2023).

Accidents: By the Numbers

In the world of texting and driving, the numbers are very startling. NHTSA's 2020 data shows that cell phone use was a factor in 13% of fatal distracted driving accidents. That's like playing a game of chance where the stakes are human lives.

The Grim Reaper's Text Message

In 2020, 396 people took their final bow because of texting and driving accidents. That's more than one per day. In

2019, it was 430. While the numbers dipped in 2020, that's still 396 too many.

The Non-Drivers' Tale

And it's not just drivers at risk. In 2019, 566 pedestrians and cyclists found themselves in the wrong place at the wrong time, thanks to distracted drivers.

Texting and Driving Deaths	
2020	396
2019	430
2018	393
2017	450
2016	496

Source: National Highway Traffic Safety Administration

Consequences of Texting and Driving

The perils of texting while driving extend far beyond the immediate risk of causing an accident. There are legal, financial, and personal ramifications that ensue, which affect not only the driver but also the general populace.

Legal Repercussions and Fines

Texting while driving is a very dangerous practice, and most states have enacted legislation banning the practice in its entirety. The sanctions for such laws range from fines and are aimed at preventing such reckless behavior. The fines differ from each state to the other and range from as low as $20 to as high as $500 or even more. However, in some states, the consequences are even more severe:

- For example, texting and driving is a criminal offense in Alaska classified as misdemeanour and attracts a jail term not exceeding one year and a fine of up to $10, 000.

- Oregon imposes fines starting at $1,000, with repeat offenders facing up to $2,500 and six months in jail for a third offense.

These laws are indicative of the fact that the threat posed by distracted driving is beginning to be understood as well as the willingness to address the issue.

Increased Risks and Penalties in Accidents

Things become much worse if texting and driving results to an accident, especially an accident that has caused people to lose their lives. In such tragic instances, the driver might have to pay the supreme price of losing license, getting arrested, or even go to jail. P. J. Miller notes that becoming involved in an accident increases the chances of putting the lives of pedestrians and road workers at risk and that the consequences of this are criminal charges rather than a simple rate increase.

Impact on Commercial Drivers

The risks are even higher for drivers of business automobiles. Currently, the use of mobile communication devices for texting by CMV drivers involved in interstate commerce is completely banned by the FMCSA. Failure to adhere to the rule can lead to severe penalties which serves to show the extent of the risk these drivers have taken given the nature of the jobs they are undertaking.

> **Random Fact:** More than 6 billion people use smartphones around the globe (Enterprise Apps Today, 2023).

Effect on Car Insurance Rates

Texting while driving does not only penalize your pocket through fines but also affects auto insurance premiums. Auto insurance providers set the premium amount by using factors such as driving records. Having a conviction for texting while driving can cause premiums to rise, often significantly, depending on the circumstances of the incident.

The comprehensive fallout from texting and driving illustrates a critical point: the temptation to turn and gaze at a phone and keep texting while driving can affect not only the individual but also society in general. It is something that should remind us all of the fact that safety is something that we all need to uphold and we need to be as keen as ever on the roads.

Fostering Positive Habits in a Digital World

It is important to keep track of the things we do in our day-to-day digital lives and how they may lead to negative consequences. While going through the impacts of distracted driving and accidents affecting pedestrians, it is about time that we shifted gears and looked at the positive side. What steps can be taken to eliminate such unhealthy habits and employ more beneficial and conscious approach to the use of digital technology? It is, therefore, right and good that we begin this journey of change.

Identifying Harmful Patterns

The first step in this change process, is to identify the maladaptive uses of technology. Ask yourself: Have you ever lifted your phone to your ear without knowing how exactly it ended up in your hand? Do you think that if you are not able to get your hands on your phone at least once every few minutes then it is not right? Are notifications always disruptive to your attention, even in dangerous conditions, for instance, while operating a vehicle?

These are not just tendencies; they are actually innate instinctive behaviors that have been developed over a given period. That little 'ding' sound has become our modern Pavlov's bell which instructs us to put everything aside and see what the phone or whatever device we are using has to offer. This reflex, especially when underlying the wheel or crossing a road, is not only dangerous but potentially lethal.

> **Random Fact:** 44% of smartphone users feel anxious when someone else uses their phone (Reviews.org, 2023).

Crafting Healthier Digital Interactions

Therefore, it is crucial to understand that breaking these patterns is not an easy task and need to be done deliberately and tactfully. Here are some actionable steps to start replacing harmful habits with positive ones:

1. **Mindful Phone Use**: Try to make a rule to be less dependent on your phone. It has been established that before you even pick up your phone, you should first ask yourself if it is necessary to use it at that particular moment, and if the answer is no, you should avoid using it.

2. **Notification Management**: You can further elaborate and specify the alerts that you want to receive. Some of the ways of avoiding interruptions include disabling unnecessary notifications which means that you are constantly interrupted by notifications. It is a simple tip that can help in reducing the frequency at which one feels compelled to look at his or her phone.

3. **Designated No-Phone Times**: There should be certain hours of the day that you choose to avoid the use of the phone intentionally. This could be when you are eating, watching TV with your family, or even when driving a car. These moments can prove useful in helping you to engage with the physical environment and decrease the amount of time spent in front of screens.

4. **Tech-Free Zones**: Ensure that there are some areas within the home that are restricted to technological gadgets such as the bedroom and dining room. It can also assist in practicing improved sleep hygiene and helps you spend more time with friends and families.

5. **Replacement Activities**: It is essential to find other activities that you can engage in to help you avoid using your phone during certain times. This could be reading a book, having a cup of coffee with a friend, listening to music, or going for a walk. The only solution is to look for an activity that is interesting and has zero relation to screens.

6. **Drive Mode Apps**: Some phones have drive mode applications or options where the phone only allows certain options to be used while in a car. Some apps

provide an auto-text response to indicate that the person is driving and will only be able to reply later.

> **Random Fact:** People use social media for 144 minutes on average each day (Enterprise Apps Today, 2023).

Action Plan:

1. **Recognize Dangerous Habits:** It is equally important to observe your behaviors that involve the use of the phone while driving or walking. To change these habits, we need to start by accepting them.

2. **Customize Notifications:** Reduce distractions by silencing notifications on the phone to reduce distractions while working.

3. **Establish No-Phone Zones:** This is due to the temptation that is associated with the use of the phone and hence implementing the no tech zones especially during the car and during meals.

4. **Use Drive Mode Apps:** This will reduce as many distractions as possible when driving, use drive mode features or apps on the phone.

Bonus Chapters:

That is correct! You are getting these TWO BONUS CHAPTERS at no additional charge, completely free, no money required!

I will preface these chapters by saying this...even though the content has absolutely nothing to do with your cell phone, I believe that they are a vital ingredient in giving you the motivation to make changes in your life.

Before you can embark on a game plan to reduce your screen time, you must have a reason for wanting to do so. There has to be some sort of 'pot of gold' sitting at the end of the rainbow, which is where these two chapters fit it.

I do realize that this book is about how to spend less time of your phone and more time "living in the moment" with the people in your life that matter most. But I think I would be remise if I didn't weave in these two bonus chapters.

The first bonus chapter dives deep into helping you craft your perfect lifestyle that brings you the most amount of fulfilment, and how to go about accomplishing your dreams.

The second chapter breaks down how to be uber efficient with how you spend your time, and how to prioritize your daily activities. Both of these skill sets are vitally important and must be on firm ground before you can attempt any Digital Detox.

Enjoy!

CHAPTER 10

Lifestyle Design

This chapter is intended to be the ultimate brainstorming session for your life.

It's about life... and doing the things that are most important. All rolled up into one tidy package for you to consume. Before we begin, I want to ask you a simple question:

If you could find a way to only work twenty-four hours a week, seven months a year, and have the rest of the time to do the things in life that are most important to you, would you be interested? My bet is that your answer is a resounding "YES!".

I call this the *NEW 24/7 Mentality,* and it has been my driving beacon for most of my adult life. For most of my career, I have tried to be so efficient with what I do that I was able to work only 24 hours a week, 7 months a year and have the rest of the time to do with as I please. It hasn't always worked out that way, but that has been the shining beacon on the hill that kept me striving for a better tomorrow.

It's been said many times before by people much smarter and wiser - and probably better looking than myself - that building a profitable business requires sacrificing everything to be counted as a successful enterprise. You will hear it from the gurus, read it in just about every business-type book, and witness it in practically every corner of the business world.

Work hard: twenty-hour days, if necessary. Sacrifice your personal time with family and friends. Put your hobbies and interests on the shelf. Be willing to give up almost everything to give your business the best chance for success. This book is *NOT* about that.

Twenty years before being a "lifestyle entrepreneur" was a thing, I was living it. For most of my adult life, I have been called a rebel, a status-quo disruptor, an innovator, and a trailblazer. It's likely because I was dropped on my head when I was young, but also because I tend to take the road less traveled in my business ventures and in life. If everyone else seems to be doing things a certain way, I'll be the guy not lined up like a lemming to follow the leader.

If the other kids were selling lemonade for 25 cents, I would be the kid selling it for 50 cents, but I would give you a free fresh-baked cookie. Always looking for the different angle.

No matter what adventure I am on, the underpinning of my motivation has always been to find ways to work less so I had more time to enjoy my life. I'm not lazy by any means; I just don't want to spend all my time working. So, I have spent most of my career looking for ways to work less and live more. That is what this book is truly about.

I am totally in love with what I do for a living, but I don't want to work anymore than I absolutely must to support the lifestyle I have built for myself. I have found that it's not necessary to spend unlimited hours immersed in my businesses to the point that I don't remember my kids' names, forget about the game, or neglect to take the car to the mechanic for a tune-up. It's not worth it.

Whether you own a business or not, anyone with a dream of placing their lifestyle before their job or business is what I call a part of the UNLEASHED TRIBE. Someone with the spirit and gumption to want a better life for themselves and their families.

I will share a vast plethora of cutting-edge ideas, some counterintuitive approaches to building your perfect life, and a few inspirational stories. This chapter will illustrate important facts about living a passionate life in charge of your own destiny.

The bottom line is this: I want you to hand-craft the perfect life for yourself and your family, work backwards, and reverse-engineer your lifestyle in order to meet those goals. This chapter will act as a blueprint on how you can do just that.

I've put in long days, long weeks, long months, and long years building brands that failed and succeeded. I did it for a distinct reason. It was all part of my master plan to create a phenomenal life.

Over the course of my journey, I built successful brands that employed wonderful people, created needed products & services for my customers, and generated tremendous profits. It's wired in my DNA, and I love the steep climb!

What Is Your CORE

There's a flame deep inside my soul, and I assume you have that same undying flame. It's the voice in my head and heart urging me on, even when there is silence. This voice constantly instills in me the desire to make a profound difference in the world for the people that I call my CORE: my family, and my closest friends.

We all have this core group at the center of our universe. It's what gives us a distinctive reason to get up each day and put on our boots.

I assume you are brimming over with the desire to become the absolute best you possibly can be. There is an innate desire to reach for goals that seem unreachable. Some are lying just below the surface, but some have been deeply buried for so long that it will take time to dig them out.

Maybe it's that dream you have of someday starting your own business, perhaps to one day travel to Australia for a month, or maybe you dream of having a small cabin on the river somewhere in the mountains where you can retire. You may have put these dreams aside because of your kids, your job, or life's emergencies. Well, guess what? The stars will never line up completely, and there is never a better time than right now to jump in with both feet.

It's human nature to have something to gravitate to all the time and to keep striving for, but it's easy to let our goals slowly slip into oblivion and become a distant memory if we aren't careful.

If someone asked us, we would readily acknowledge that we want life to be exciting, but some of us have gotten too comfortable and content sitting on the couch. We need a challenge, but only a few of us ever dare to follow our hearts.

We all share a common passion for what we do. That is the American Dream at full strength!

There's a new belief system that is taking the world by storm, and it's a philosophy that is flipping traditional lifestyle models on their heads.

It's a group of people that put their families and personal lifestyle choices first, then build their income blueprints based on these choices. This progressive trend exemplifies a reverse hierarchy of traditional goal setting. It redefines what it means to have a successful life.

To many traditional-thinking people, this type of thinking leads to doom and gloom. They wonder how you can survive unless you put your job and career at the top of the food chain.

If you are part of the Unleashed Tribe like myself, setting such outdated and outrageous goals are secondary to attaining the satisfaction I get from spending time with my family, personal projects, and rewarding lifestyle activities.

If It's Not a "Hell Yes," Then It's a "Big Fat No!"

If something doesn't help me to attain my ultimate lifestyle goals, I take a pass on it. I am constantly asked to sit on company boards, invited to sit in meetings that have no relevance to my ultimate objectives, or encouraged to take on projects that will only "slow my roll" and not lead to a better life. I do my fair share of volunteering and give plenty to charities, but I do NOT want to be that guy that says "yes" to everything. I constantly ask myself if the activity will help me achieve my ultimate goals.

Basically, if it's not a "HELL YES", then it must be a "BIG FAT NO!"

Your default answer to all new tasks or activities that require your attention must be "NO." End of discussion. More on this later.

When I began thinking this way, I recalibrated the way that I approached creative problem solving and found innovative, out-of-the-box solutions. Sadly, most people have no reason to think like this unless they are faced with a devastating event.

This inverse strategy keeps my mind focused on priorities I value, while also giving me a laser-focused approach to getting my work done quickly and efficiently.

I'm decorated with honor badges of trial-and-error, massive setbacks, and victories, but I've always been a willing participant in the process.

I've lived the better part of my life with this simple yet highly effective approach.

What Kills Passion

These skills are sometimes inherently inside of you, but often must be nurtured and developed over time and must come with a dose of passion and purpose.

However, purpose and motivation don't strike us like lightning. These good habits must be cultivated through practice and patience. The exuberant enthusiasm that seeps from every cell of your body is not a feeling or a mood. You must act.

Let's discuss some common deterrents preventing us from unleashing our full potential.

Procrastination

I believe the biggest killer of our motivation and passion is procrastination. This unfortunate malaise is caused by our misunderstanding that doing certain tasks will cause us some sort of pain.

Against that perceived pain, we must balance the enormous benefits.

Do any of these thoughts sound familiar?

- I'll get to it TOMORROW!
- I'll take the kids to the park NEXT weekend.
- I'll make that trip to Alaska when I retire.
- Maybe when I'm older.
- Perhaps when I'm more settled in my job.
- Maybe when the kids are out of the house.
- I'll buy that big TV I've been wanting for the last two years as soon as the old one breaks down.

What if that day never comes? No matter what your circumstances are in life, you will always come up with reasons why something can't be done. Instead, why not come up with ONE great reason why you should?

Procrastination can be the great robber of our time if we're not careful. Nothing will suck out the vigor for life faster than a good case of it. Show me a garage stuffed with "I'll get to it later" projects, and I'll show you a life that is not reaching its full potential. Nothing can stop a dream faster than our own laziness.

Well, today is the first day of the rest of your life. You can begin now to take control of your life and get back to that feeling of relevance and contentment.

Check out this piece of anonymous wisdom about procrastination:

They were going to be all that they wanted to be... tomorrow.

None would be braver or kinder than they... tomorrow.

A friend who was troubled and weary, they knew, would be glad of a lift— and needed it too.

On him, they would call—see what they could do... tomorrow.

Each morning they stacked up the letters they'd write... tomorrow. The greatest of people they just might have been, the world would have opened its heart to them.

But, in fact, they passed on and faded from view, and all that they left when their living was through was a mountain of things, they intended to do... tomorrow.

I can't impress upon you enough that you must act today. If you can't see yourself realizing the dream, you never will. Just when you're about ready to succeed, something will surely pull you back. If you feel overwhelmed, break it down and get started.

After all, you can't eat an elephant all at once, can you? Start breaking down the big things in your life into small, manageable tasks to eat one bite at a time.

Ah, but there's always tomorrow, right?

Working Hard or Smart?

How many people do you know that work two or even three jobs, yet still struggle to make ends meet? Heck, maybe you're one of those people.

Working hard is admirable, but it won't make you a fortune or happy in the long run. It might have worked for the older generations like the Silent Generation, Baby Boomers, and even some Gen X's, but in this day and age, that paradigm is obsolete.

Today is about working smart – regardless of the invested hours. Plus, working smart means fewer doctor's appointments in a futile attempt to fix that damaged spine, hypertension, or high cholesterol—all caused by overexposure to the modern day's stress and anxiety.

But what does it mean to work smart rather than hard? In a nutshell, working smart means investing your full capacities in the most profitable segments of your operations and delegating everything else.

Things that are certain hypes these days like micromanaging and multitasking don't belong to the concept of smart work.

Take retail day traders. These guys commonly make six or seven figures a year without even blinking, let alone investing some hard labor into it. Their trick is looking into the future.

A whole army of analysts prepares daily, weekly, monthly, and Y-on-Y reports, but a trader simply decides whether to go long or short. His only concern is the future. The army dwells on the past and present situation.

Or take me. Three-plus successful businesses, having 2 radio shows that are heard on over 100 radio stations across the country, blending my public speaking and writing in with my work schedule...you would think that I don't even have the time to brush my teeth, let alone play catch with my son, take my oldest daughter shopping and to lunch or play Sky Dragons with my youngest.

You just need to let go of one common, well-rooted dogma that society and your parents planted in your mind while you were just a kid, that working long hours at your job is a virtue.

Balancing Private and Professional

Now, if you really aren't concerned about anything outside of your work endeavors, that's completely ok. You have my permission to put this book down and return to your unending work.

On the other hand, if you are a human being who needs support from your loved ones, hear me out now and hear me well.

By far, the most important asset that you and I possess is time, and the biggest decision we have daily is how we choose to spend it.

We have 86,400 seconds each day. How we consciously choose to spend those seconds determines who we ultimately become over a lifetime.

Each day, we literally make hundreds of decisions that determine what kinds of successes or failures our businesses will endure. Many of these seconds, minutes, and hours are wasted on thoughts and activities that add zero value to our lives or the lives of the people who mean the most to us. And once that time is spent, we can never get it back.

Leaving my corporate job back in 1994 provided a real shock to my system. The School of Hard Knocks was about to open its doors to me. If I didn't do it correctly, there would be a deep grave of failed business corpses waiting at the end of the proverbial hallway of doom.

I knew my chances of success were low. I was aware half of all businesses ended within their first year, 80% were gone within five years, and 96% failed within 10 years. I had started and built several businesses before then, but this was the first time I was going to be all in with no fallback. For those of you who have started a business at some point in your life, you know exactly what I'm talking about.

Even with doom and gloom staring at me in the face, my only thought was: *Hooray, I'm going to be one of the 4% who will make it as an entrepreneur!*

There's an excitement that wells up inside. A surreal calm that overtakes the inner fears of the prospective businessperson. In fact, the excitement can be so magnificent that it's difficult to shut off the river of creative ideas flowing at every waking moment of the day.

I knew my odds were low, but I had a big advantage over failure. I had the rare ability to live EVERY DAY LIKE A SATURDAY!

In other words, I don't get the Monday morning blues or get stuck in the rut of a nine-to-five work week mentality.

The Awakening

This life-changing philosophy was instilled in me by my stepfather, Pat Wright, one of the hardest working men I've ever met. He loved my mom deeply, and that motivated him to do whatever was necessary to keep us safe and secure.

You see, my parents divorced when I was eleven, and my mom worked two or three jobs at a time to provide for my brother, sister, and me. We would see Dad on weekends, but the day-to-day raising of us kids was all Mom. Pat came into our lives several years later, and by that time we were a tribe of hardened souls accustomed to doing without in many cases, but never lacking in the important things in life.

When I was in my early 20s, Mom and Pat dreamed of owning a boat. Not a big, fancy boat to sail the seven seas in, but a boat the family could take to Hayden Lake in North Idaho where we could spend our weekends floating off into the warm summer evenings.

With this dream in mind, they managed to set aside enough money to realize their dream. They eventually found and bought Big Red, an old V-hulled Fiberform. The excitement in our family was incredibly palpable. She was an older vessel that needed a paint job and some TLC, but she had class.

We bought Pat his very first captain's hat, loaded the cooler with beer and water, and set sail.

I distinctly remember to this day how the five of us left the marina with smiles in tow on a beautiful summer day. With our troubles behind us, we fell into total silence as we looked around and gazed at the beautiful mountains and shorelines. We were without a care in the world. Nobody was going to take away the beauty of that moment from us.

The awesome silence was broken by Pat's immortal words: "I wonder what the poor folk are doing today."

Those words hit home. We suddenly felt elevated to a higher plane at that singular moment. We were all in Never-Never Land for that tiny little slice of our awesome day that nobody could take away from us. An amazing feeling of euphoria floated in our minds, however fleeting.

"Babe, we are the poor folk," my mother responded.

Her words were true to the core in the practical sense, but practicality was out the window that day.

Pat affectionately looked at each of us, then looked out to the horizon with his chest puffed up and his head held high.

"Not today, Babe," he said. "Not today."

At that precise moment, we became the richest people on planet Earth—and it had nothing to do with money.

You can have all the money in the world, but it won't matter if you don't have someone precious to share it with. And that's exactly what will happen if you let your professional life take over.

Those brief moments of joy we feel every time a child smiles from the deepest depths of his heart, or erotic arousal when our partner slowly leans on us are all we've got. Someday, not so far from now, you'll find yourself sitting in a chair, in front of a window, remembering. Those few reminiscences will be all you have left. Did you build an environment potent enough to create an emotion so powerful that it can create a long-lasting memory? A single memory that could trigger joy and excitement once again even decades after?

Whether you like it or not, one thing will always tip the scale and it's up to you to decide which one it will be.

The Disruptive 24/7 Paradigm

The Unleashed Tribe members work diligently to reinvent the ways in which they put their life together, and how they approach what they do for a living. In living a balanced life, they want to:

- Work smarter so they can spend more time doing OTHER THINGS.

- Work less so they can spend more time doing OTHER THINGS.

- Reinvent how they run their businesses so they can spend more time doing OTHER THINGS.

To sum up, they basically wanted to work less and live more.

I've always approached my life like a bull in a China shop. But one thing I can say about my philosophy of *"Making Every Day A Saturday"* is that you only live this life once, so you'd better make it count.

The zeal for living that I've always possessed deep in my gut has fueled me for as long as I can remember. I became determined not to become a prisoner to my businesses, but to live life like I really meant it. Now, it's time for you to pull the same prank on the system and established paradigms.

As I mentioned earlier, I have a "24/7 Mentality," but not in the way you have believed your entire life. When you hear "24/7," what do you immediately think of?

Most people think of twenty-four hours a day, seven days a week. This typically refers to someone who keeps his or her nose to the grindstone all the time, or a business that never closes, right?

Does this sound like anyone you know? I believe this describes a large population in the world these days. However, my definition of the 24/7-work mentality is quite different.

To me, it means twenty-four hours a week, seven months a year. Let that soak in a minute. Let me ask you an especially important question- If there was a way for you to work only 24 hours a week, 7 months a year, and you had the rest of the time to do with whatever you pleased…would that be of interest to you? Think about that question as you move through this book.

EXERCISE: Building Your "Perfect Day"

A potter knows that to end up with something worthwhile, they must know what they are making ahead of time. If you simply threw the lump of clay onto the potter's wheel without knowing what you wanted to make, you'd end up with the same lump. You must have an idea of what you're trying to accomplish before you begin the process of formation and transformation.

Likewise, the caterpillar's calling to become a butterfly means it must strain, grow, stretch, and change within the confines of its chrysalis. Before it emerges from its sheltered cocoon and flies away, the caterpillar must struggle and strain to get out of its prison and fulfill its destiny. It's a process to grow and mature. Just like the caterpillar, you're not meant to stay inside a cocoon forever. You're meant to fly!

With that said, the process of imagining "a perfect lifestyle" can give us leeway to craft "a perfect day."

To be able to work twenty-four hours a week, seven months a year, and use the rest of your time to do whatever is important to you, you'll have to radically change the way you approach your business. You'll need to deconstruct your preconceived notions of what success means on the deepest levels. Would you be a willing participant in this process if you knew there was a pot of gold waiting for you at the end of the virtual rainbow? Sure, you would.

Start With The End, And End With The Beginning

Let me tell you what a perfect day is for me. I would wake up at 4:00 AM, feeling refreshed both physically and emotionally. After spending time outside with my dogs, Tilly & Delilah, I'd enjoy a fresh-brewed cup of good coffee with half-and-half and honey.

The table next to my recliner would be piled high with books and magazines that I'd be ecstatic to dive into. I'd have some new-age jazz, classic rock, or a podcast playing away in my headphones. Once I checked my sports scores, the news, and weather for the day, I'd spend the first two hours immersed in self-improvement activities to get my juices flowing. All private time with no interruptions.

The next hour would be spent in the REFLEX ZONE responding to the world's requests for my time. I'd reply to emails, honey-do lists, and other activities centered on the demands on my time from outside sources.

After that, I'd wake my kids from their night's slumber and help them get ready for their day. Daddy bonding time would be a precious way of getting to know them just a little bit better before the day began for us.

I would send each off to school with the biggest hug in the world, and an amazing affirmation of, "I LOVE YOU TO MARS AND BACK TIMES INFINITY PLUS TEN!" They would know beyond a doubt their Daddy loves them more than any other Daddy has ever loved their kids.

Then, it would be time to go to work. During my pre-planned work hours, I'd be uber-efficient with my responsibilities, such as making calls, writing projects, team meetings & training, product evaluations, recording my radio shows, and so on.

All these activities would be put into a "POD." In my definition, it means a section of time dedicated to a singular task or series of similar tasks without the influence of outside forces. We will talk more about the POD system a bit later.

I want to have the best time anyone can legally have while working. Remember, I love what I do so much that I believe I haven't worked a single day since the spring of 1994, so it's amazingly easy for me to imagine this. Short, sweet, and to the point. I would get maximum results for minimal amounts of effort expended. Work time done, back to the fun.

There'd be a fishing pole and a pack of night crawlers waiting for me as soon as I was done working, I'd spend an hour catching the biggest trout you ever saw! The fish would put up a great fight before finally being defeated by my outstanding fishing skills. On the way home, I'd have inspiring phone conversations with my mom, and my dad.

By the time I got home, the kids would be getting off the school bus. I'd proceed to hear about their day's activities and help them with homework.

We would then adjourn to the kitchen to prepare a delicious five-course meal, each member of the family preparing a course that would fit in with our chosen culinary theme.

After dinner, a family board game or some guitar playing, playing with our dogs Tilly & Delilah, playing catch with my son, listening to my daughter's new songs in her playlist, and reading a book with my youngest. Laughing until my sides hurt, then more laughing, then laughing some more.

After shower and reading time, it would be bedtime for all all of us, and a short review of your day. I would try to squeeze just a few more minutes and moments of happiness out of them.

Then, I'd head downstairs to finish up with any incomplete projects for the day, and cap it all off with a relaxing sauna and a hot shower. Lastly, I'd read in bed until I slowly drifted off into slumber for the night.

What a perfect day that would be. All my favorite people and experiences rolled up into a single day.

Does it sound too simple? Maybe. Then again, I can tell you that it happens on a regular basis in my life. I have a perfect day ALL THE TIME!

I call these type of perfect days **"LEVEL I"** days. It's a day I love replicating repeatedly, and they have become the cornerstone of my own perfect lifestyle. Such days are filled with the people and things I love, and outcomes I can anticipate. Do these days have setbacks and surprises? Absolutely. But I try to be flexible and roll with the adversity and unexpected surprises.

If I keep the big picture in mind, the perfect day seems to work itself out, even with occasional bumps along the road. My bar is set at a level where I know I can be successful consistently, instead of setting myself up for failure.

All too often, people set the bar so high that it would take a few miracles to achieve success at any level. It makes much better sense to reward yourself with mini victories along the way, doesn't it?

I have other types of perfect days as well.

LEVEL II includes achievable goals, events, and experiences that can't be replicated every day, such as:

- Watching a championship game with any of my teams playing: the LA Dodgers, Angels, Lakers, USC Trojans, UCLA Bruins, LA Kings, Colorado State Rams, Gonzaga Bulldogs, the Arkansas Razorbacks, or John Daly the golfer. Unfortunately, many of my teams don't make it to their respective championship games, but I'm a true fan. I hurt for days, even weeks when we lose a tough game. But I keep the dream alive 365 days a year! Sports fans, you know exactly what I'm talking about. Win or lose, we're their biggest fans!

- Attending a concert by one of my favorite artists.

- Spending a holiday celebration with my immediate family.

- Launching a new product or service for one of my companies.

- Giving a seminar to a large group of hungry entrepreneurs and hearing about their successes.

- Spend the entire day in a workshop networking with other likeminded UEs.

- Hitting annual sales projections.

- Taking the motorhome on a mini vacation to the mountains and finding a secluded spot.

LEVEL III perfect days are goals, events, and experiences that require extensive planning, discipline, and commitment, such as:

- Hanging out on the beach in Mexico for a month without a single thing to do except eat and scuba dive.

- Taking a month off with the motorhome and living in the mountains, waking up every morning to the sound of a rushing river and singing birds.

- Buying or selling a business.

- Being with my kids when they reach lifetime milestone markers, such as their first steps, first day out of diapers, first straight-A report card, first time driving, graduation, weddings, and the birth of every grandchild.

I could go on for an entire chapter listing the different types of perfect days, but I think you get the point.

These are individual events that happen in life, but I have created the vision in my mind of how a perfect day can be built around these activities. I want to have perfect days all the time! I work hard to keep that vision strongly embedded in my brain.

I want my life to be filled with the best days ever, one right after the next. I don't mind meeting and overcoming setbacks that stand in the way because I know the best things in life require a little pain on occasion.

You may look at my day as a simpleton at work, and I thank you for the compliment. I am passionate about the pursuit of happiness in my life; this has become the cornerstone of what a perfect day means to me. I suggest you seriously consider this core idea for your emotional health and the health of your business.

We each have a different ideal lifestyle, and that is great. Your day is unique to you and nobody else in the universe.

I genuinely believe I can have perfect days. I also believe you can experience them as well.

Does this sound counter-intuitive to the way you're used to setting goals or taking on challenges? To truly live the unleashed life, this step is a vital piece to the puzzle, as you'll discover.

Our lives are made up of dreams, goals, aspirations, wants, desires, and unmitigated passions. Many of us may talk a good game, but we tend to fumble the ball on the five-yard line when it comes to the follow-through.

Don't feel bad if this sounds like you. The world is full of people who have a difficult time finishing what they start. It's extremely easy to get sidetracked or lose focus on the goals we have set, especially with endless forces vying for our time and attention. The sad part is we have allowed our time to be hijacked right in front of our very eyes.

Success is achieved with a series of mini steps that will ultimately take you to the finish line. You're basically planning and working backwards with your entire life, which will then give you the vision of what needs to get done.

Let's say that tomorrow you can have the best day of your life. No rules, no limitations. When you go to bed tonight, you know tomorrow will be your ideal day. Would that change your perspective on how you approached the day?

Crafting Your Perfect Day

Before we begin, when was the last time you remember having a perfect day? How many perfect days have you had over this past week, month, or year? How do they make you feel? Are you having a tough time coming up with answers quickly?

As we create your "Holy Grail Day," you'll need to consciously try not to let emotions and routines get in your way of building your new house. We're bulldozing your current lifestyle all the way down to the foundation, throwing out your preconceived notions of what total contentment means to you, and rebuilding with a much better frame.

To begin, ask the following questions, reflect on your answers, and write them all down.

- What would your perfect day look like to you?
- What activities would you do?
- Where would you go?
- Who would accompany you?
- What kinds of food would you eat?
- What music would you play in the background?

- Would you volunteer or give back to the community in any way?
- What new skill would you learn?
- Most importantly, how would this special day make you feel?
- Is this a feeling you want to experience more of in your life?
- Is this day achievable and realistic?
- Can you create this day within the structure of your current life? I'm hoping you give it an emphatic yes!

You now have created the Holy Grail Day on paper for yourself, and that's a big deal in my book!

Let's stretch out this exercise and turn your perfect day into the perfect lifestyle. Would you do the same things or add some additional ingredients to your recipe? Do NOT allow yourself to feel guilty because you are indulging yourself. This is YOUR time, and nobody can tell you otherwise. Keep in mind what your overall lifestyle goals are while you're doing this.

Please write it all down in your journal or on note cards. Everything from A-to-Z. Let your imagination run wild and your pen run out of ink.

- Where would you live?

- What kind of house would you have?

- What kind of car would you like to drive?

- Where would you go on vacation?

- What new projects or businesses would you start?

- What workshops or courses would you attend?

- What nonprofit or charity help would you like to do?

- How would you give back to your community in time and/or money?

- How much money would you set aside for retirement, second homes, college tuitions, a private jet, property in Montana, or whatever else you might want?

Allow yourself to have the creative freedom to authentically set these aspirations and goals. Unless you dream it, you'll never achieve it.

Ask yourself these and many more questions as you slowly create your masterpiece. Maybe you are already living the perfect life and that is very possible. To you, I say congratulations and a job well done! If not, we have a little more work to do. Make sure you are writing down your thoughts and answers.

Now, here's the tough question. To make this life possible, what kind of income would you need to generate from your job, business, or both?

If you've already achieved this figure, congratulations! You are the proud owner of the perfect lifestyle, and you didn't even know it. You are now one step closer to living the life of your dreams.

But if that number is beyond where you are now with your income, you'll need to reverse-engineer and restructure your business to attain your perfect life.

This is a book about putting value in your dreams, getting control of your time, and crafting a better life for yourself and your family while running a profitable business.

Now you have some guidelines for what you would like your life to look like from close range and at a distance.

Designing your perfect life can be one of the most enjoyable experiences you'll ever explore. It allows you to get to know yourself on an intimate level and will give your business a world-class jolt of adrenaline. It will not be easy by any stretch of your imagination, but that's why very few people are entrepreneurs.

I believe our ability to ask and work through difficult questions about how we view the world is an absolute must if we want to reap the benefits of thinking like a true UE.

First, envision and set your goals. Painting the masterpiece that is your life needs a healthy dose of creative thinking, followed by reverse-engineering your business and setting goals to help you achieve that vision. There is no quick fix that will give you the success you dream of, but there are simple questions you can ask yourself to shake the bushes and keep the cobwebs from creeping into your brain.

As we have discussed in detail, designing your perfect lifestyle is a matter of perspective and philosophy. It's much more than the car you drive, the house in which you live, or the amount of money in your 401k.

It's about gaining control over your precious time, so you can enjoy each special moment that comes your way without distractions.

It takes an incredibly special person to keep their nose to the grindstone each day. My goal for you is that you'll begin to replace negative habits in your life with positive, productive habits that will ignite your dreams like never before.

POPCORN EXERCISE

I call this the Popcorn Exercise. At the end of the process, you will have a firm grasp on everything that is inside of your Life Warehouse. The more information you have about yourself, the better equipped you will be to create the kind of life that you have always wanted.

We need to be acutely aware of who we are and what motivates us. That is why spending time with yourself is an important part of your daily routine. Grab a pen, a notepad, a good cup of coffee, and hit your back deck for a while.

You are going to break your life down into three categories: Personal, Family, and Professional. This exercise intends to get your life onto a piece of paper:

Personal

- Do you get upset at yourself for not sticking to your diet and exercise program? Describe what your current diet and exercise routines are, then write a new plan with new routines you will begin.

- Are you satisfied with your spiritual growth? Do you attend church services as much as you would like? If you are not religious, do you budget adequate personal or alone time so you're in touch with your internal voice? Write out a plan for your personal development.

- What hobbies are you involved in? Do you spend as much time as you would like to participate in them? Write out a plan for what activities you would like to pursue.

- Have you given up some of your passions because of children or career? Would you want to make them part of your life again?

- What do you like about yourself? How can you improve on those things?

- What don't you like about yourself? How can you improve on those things?

The purpose of the Popcorn Exercise is to "rattle your brain" a little and remove the cobwebs. Once you have brainstormed about your life as it exists today, it's time to give some thought about where you want your life to be tomorrow and begin building your perfect lifestyle.

Brainstorm For A Breakthrough

You have already handcrafted your perfect lifestyle, so now it's time to set goals in order to make that happen. Grab a stack of 3x5 index cards and let the creative juices flow! You are going to write down your personal and professional goals for the next 12 months. Your personal goals should be done before the others. You started this process earlier, so it should be easy to add to your chicken scratches and notes.

Do you want to take a vacation this year? Do you have your eye on a special boat or set of golf clubs? How about your garden? Would you like to spend more time cultivating it or working in the yard?

What about other hobbies you haven't had time for recently? If it's important to you, then you should make the time in your schedule to read, write, paint, or play with the family dog.

Write down one goal per note card. What projects have you been meaning to start or finish? Where do you want to be in one month, three months, a year, or five years? What new hobbies do you want to learn? What old hobbies and interests would you like to bring back into your life? What projects have you been putting off because you just didn't have the time? Where do you want to go on vacation? What about your family? Would you like to spend more quality time with each of them individually? Write it all down on a note card. This is the next step towards designing your perfect lifestyle.

You may have an entire stack of things you've been meaning to get to but have not dedicated the necessary time.

This exercise must be done at a time and place where you won't be interrupted or distracted. By spending just fifteen minutes a day immersed in setting goals for your life and brainstorming, you will begin to create positive habits that will stick with you for the rest of your life. Once you come up with an idea, write it down. After you put it on paper, it will be much easier to expand the idea and develop it into creative breakthroughs.

Prioritize (The Salsa Box)

Now it's time to prioritize and organize your goals. If you tried to complete everything in your stack, I venture to say you would fail miserably and feel disgusted with yourself in the process. Instead of eating the whole pizza all at once, you need to eat one slice at a time, so set some realistic goals.

Categorize your goals into three groups, like Level I, Level II, and Level III perfect days. Goals or projects that you can't wait to get started on can be placed into the "hot" section of your salsa box. Items that are a little more long-term can be put into the "medium" category. Lastly, things that are long-term can be put into the "mild" section.

Your "Salsa Box" goals will make it easier to establish some realistic timelines. By having everything already written down in your Salsa Box, you will increase your chances of success.

Share

If you want to truly make a difference in your life, you must become accountable to at least one other living person. It may be your spouse, your business partner, or your best friend, but it should be someone who understands and supports you. Set a time where you can lay out your game plan and share your goals and aspirations with them.

Ask the other person to make sure to hold your feet to the fire on occasion so you don't get lazy. If you set up a weekly conversation with them to discuss how things are going, you will allow the other person to be involved with your efforts in a very personal way.

Take Action

Once you have established your list of goals and shared them with a confidant, it's time to put your money where your mouth is. Putting some of your goals into motion can be a revolutionary step! Don't make up excuses or come up with reasons why you can't do something. Just go and get it done.

As you put this program into action and begin to emulate passionate successful people, choose something small that you will be able to accomplish easily. Dedicate yourself to doing it every day for one week.

Maybe it's something as simple as going for a short walk at lunch, spending thirty minutes a day reading self-improvement books, working on sales projections for next quarter, going through boxes in your basement, or stopping on the way home to visit a friend who's been feeling down lately.

Once you begin to make these small items part of your daily routine, the bigger things won't seem quite so daunting and overwhelming. The smallest things can make the biggest difference.

Self-Doubt And Limited Ambition

Limited ambition is another obstacle to the UE life. Dreams should be just a little bit out of reach, but not out of sight. Otherwise, they wouldn't be dreams, would they? If your dreams exceed your self-image, you'll likely do something stupid to sabotage that dream.

Earlier in my business life, I sabotaged many projects and got in the way of my own success. Ultimately, my self-doubt over- whelmed my desire to succeed. Once I learned to get out of my own way, my business fortunes changed.

Imagine that when you wake up tomorrow, everything you do will be done to the best of your ability. You'll give 110% effort to each activity you've planned for your day and disregard any fears you may have.

No obstacles. No negative thinking. No procrastination. Do you think this attitude will impact how your day turns out?

Resistance To Change

We're all creatures of habit, preferring to be comfortable with daily routines. Do you consider change wonderful and exciting, as long as it's happening to someone else?

Life is in a constant state of flux, so we tend to gravitate towards our comfort zones. It seems too risky to try something new.

Comfort zones are neither good nor bad, but most people mistakenly think they perform their best when they are in a safe and familiar place.

I truly dislike being comfortable. If it gets to be too much, I'll create some chaos and shake up my world a bit. I get extremely bored with my life if my daily routines begin to feel "always the same." It drives me to the point at which I must either create a new product, start a new business, buy a new business, or completely shake up my routines.

No matter how enthusiastic you are, you'll stagnate if you don't take responsibility in your job, marriage, friendships, and hobbies. Anything not making progress is on its way to becoming stagnant and boring, which is to be avoided when pursuing and embracing our lives with passion as successful UEs.

Here are some exercises that can help shake the bushes of your life:

- Try a new restaurant this week. I challenge you to try a cuisine you're unaccustomed to.

- Buy different brands at the grocery store, such as deodorant, toothpaste, or dish soap.

- Take a new route to work. Be pleasantly surprised at how much beauty there is out there.

- Listen to a style of music you typically don't listen to. Scan your radio for a new station to listen to.

- Sample a different dinner recipe for seven straight nights. Google and research recipes and add the ingredients to your weekly shopping list. Give your culinary palate a shake up!

- Read a book completely out of your comfort zone.

- Switch the side of the bed you sleep on. You may have to sweet-talk your spouse or significant other, but you'll be amazed how different it makes you feel.

- If you have longer hair, try a different hairstyle, or add some color.

- Pick an obscure subject you know little about. Research and read about it, watch videos on it, then write a five-hundred-word essay. Don't worry about making it sound like a Pulitzer prize-winning document. Just pour your heart and effort into making it the best report you've ever written.

- Eat and write with your opposite hand for twenty-four hours. Don't worry about dropped spaghetti. Practice writing your name twenty-five times and see how much you can improve. This exercise activates the opposite side of your brain, rewarding you with an enormously powerful sensation after a short time. I try this technique two-to-three times a week, just to keep things a little off-centered.

- Instead of salting your food, try seasonings like salad dressings, hot sauces, pepper, BBQ sauces, vinegars, and spices for flavor. Make this a fun project and see what kinds of flavors stimulate your taste buds.

If you keep doing what you have always done, you'll keep getting what you've always gotten. It'll be virtually impossible to break out of your mental funk unless you shake up your mental branches to stimulate your foggy brain.

As Albert Einstein noted, "We cannot solve our problems with the same thinking we used when we created them."

Take a risk! You might not like it, but you'll never know unless you try.

If you step up to the plate, you might strike out. If you don't try, you'll never know the true joy of hitting a home run. Barry Bonds struck out over fifteen hundred times during his career, but he has also hit more home runs than anyone else in Major League Baseball history.

When you take a risk or face a fear, you move forward with your life. Eventually, you will become successful. As challenging as it may sound, this is a simple formula in living life to the fullest.

Here's another problem with comfort zones. If you're good, staying comfy can keep you from becoming great. That in and of itself should motivate you to get off your butt!

A Lack Of Discipline

Show me a successful businessperson, and I'll show you someone who is disciplined and dedicated to his or her mission. Success and failure are habits and self-fulfilling prophecies. If you don't prioritize and build positive habits, you will just stagnate and create your own demise.

In high school, I competed in the 400-meter dash on a national level and became an All-American. Between my coach, parents, friends, and competition, I was able to create an extraordinarily strong set of goals I wanted to accomplish with my running. At one point, my times were on track to qualify for the U.S. Olympic Trials in Eugene, Oregon. Unfortunately, a torn hamstring ended my college sprinting career, forcing me into retirement long before I was ready.

But that experience left an indelible lifelong impact. Athletics is a powerful way to learn about self-discipline and setting goals. I know that my core values and beliefs are firmly rooted in the training I received from competitive sports.

Do you wait to see how you feel before making plans? Are you easily sidetracked, or do you have a sense of discipline? The key to staying focused and dedicated isn't hard if it's something you love and are passionate about.

Any discipline you desire must be built up gradually. If your goal is to run a marathon next year, you can't start out by running twenty-six miles on your first day of training. Start small and work your way up.

Fear

Our innate fear of trying something new has been part of human nature since the dawn of civilization. We tend to avoid any kind of risk if it has anything to do with taking us out of our comfort zone.

Fear stops many people from taking risks. If we aren't willing to walk out on a limb, we'll never get to the best fruit that the tree of life has to offer.

Overcoming our fear is how we learn to do just about everything in our lives, such as eating different foods for the first time, driving a car, talking to strangers, speaking up at meetings, or playing catch with our kids. They all come with certain levels of risk.

Trying a new variety of apple and investing $1,000,000 into a new business are both risky in their own unique ways. As humans, we like to take "measured" risks, meaning we can mitigate what may happen to us.

Pessimists and negative thinkers say things like *You might get struck by lightning if you go outside*, or *did you know over one hundred people a day are killed in car wrecks in the US, which means I shouldn't drive?* Boy, what a waste of a person's great potential and mind space to think so negatively.

Nobody likes to lose, but there's no loss in going for it at all. The only loss in not trying is not having gone for it.

How do you overcome negative talk with yourself and people you meet? If you are unable to convince these people to be more open to having a positive outlook, then it's time to move on. Life is too short to allow yourself to be surrounded with people who attempt to bring you down, whether it's unintentional or not.

It's completely cool to surround yourself with people who espouse ideas opposite to yours. This can open your thinking to new ideas and creative problem solving, but negative thinking has no place in your 86,400-second day.

Setting Goals

In my business life, I am ruthless. I'm an extremely aggressive marketer, an above average salesperson who knows how to close, and I find niches in the marketplace that are not being occupied by others. I know how to focus on my superpowers and squeeze out every drop of potential to win.

I delegate 80% of my daily tasks that bring only 20% of my results, leaving me with the 20% of my time to focus on the right tasks that bring 80% of my positive results. If you give me a brand-new business, I am confident that I will have that brand sailing towards the top of the food chain within six months. I would do this in part by offloading what I would call the second-tier activities, which allows me to focus on getting the biggest return on my time investment.

I temper this confident attitude with a much more subdued approach in my personal life. Because I am dedicated to having my perfect lifestyle at the top of the pyramid, it makes me more dedicated to getting my work done as quickly and efficiently as possible.

In looking back on my business journey, the takeaway for you should be to use common sense. If you have a laser-beam focus on your goals, priorities, and time, you can revolutionize your business blueprint. My businesses are constrained by design. I may have the mindset of a millionaire, but that doesn't mean that I must relinquish control over my life to attain that status.

Let's proceed with a simple exercise that will start defining some of your personal and professional goals, which will ultimately lead to the master plan for your perfect lifestyle. Don't worry about the money aspect for now. Just answer these questions honestly and be sure to write down your answers. Simply writing down your thoughts and goals is more effective in communicating with your subconscious to better achieve your aspirations.

Have fun playing and imagining your dream lifestyle.

If you had a magic wand:

- How many days off a week would you like?

- What will you do with your free time?

- Where would you like to travel?

- What hobbies would you like to spend more time on?

- What kind of car do you want to drive?

- What kinds of clothes do you want to wear?

- What kind of house do you want to live in?

- Which relationships are most important to you, and how can you nurture them?

- What would you change about yourself for self-improvement?

We'll call this perfect lifestyle list the Holy Grail since it contains all the shiny objects in the sky you'll always be striving for as a UE.

Now, here is the challenging part. You need to come up with a grand total dollar amount. How much will it take to comfortably sustain your vision for the Holy Grail? You have now started to paint a picture of your perfect lifestyle.

Deciding on what you want is the first step towards getting it. Our thoughts determine the direction of our lives. Life is more about the journey than the destination. If you change your thinking, you can change your life.

Harness Your Mental Power To Imagine Success

Imagine a big, juicy lemon sitting on the table in front of you. Grab a knife and cut it into wedges. With your mind's eye, smell the citrus wafting through the room. The refreshing scent fills the air with bursts of new energy to revitalize your senses. Still in your mind's eye, take a wedge, take a huge bite, and suck the wedge until all the juice is completely in your mouth. Very sour, isn't it?

Are you salivating? This is how the power of words affects and engages us emotionally. Words are simple tools that enable us to create dreams, including that amazing vision of where you want to be in your life.

Do you have a vision of how you want your life to be? Is your dream embedded in your brain in a way that is so compelling that it drives you to where you need to be? Is it as sensory as the cut lemon and refreshing aroma wafting through all your senses?

Your mind is an incredibly powerful tool in helping you achieve goals and grab your slices of happiness.

We've been taught to believe that our dreams are not meant to come true and that dreaming takes us away from tasks at hand. People accused of being daydreamers are thought to be lazy, foolish, or not plugged into reality.

And yet, how would things have ever gotten done if we didn't imagine the results beforehand? If Thomas Edison had not tried, failed, and retried over 6,000 times, we would not have the benefit of electric light bulbs today.

Daydreaming is key to sharpening your focus on what you really want. Every invention and every great new idea were birthed at one time by people who daydreamed. I've been accused of being a daydreamer for much of my life, but I can honestly say that many of my "aha" bright ideas have been the result of my mind being allowed to wander off into the great unknown.

Once upon a time, there was a man living in a cold cave who daydreamed about making fire to stay warm, but it took us over one million years to figure out how to utilize it. Someone daydreamed about inventing ice cream over four thousand years ago, but it wasn't until only over a hundred years ago that someone came up with the idea for the ice cream cone. In 1775, the flush toilet was invented, followed eighty-two years later by the invention of toilet paper!

The world goes around because of people who daydreamed, imagined, and strongly believed they could make the world a better place for themselves and others.

You're never too young or too old to dream big dreams. Figure out what's holding you back from designing the life of your dreams and then forge ahead.

Taking Responsibility

We all have times in which we feel like the world is out to get us. I remember events in my life when it seemed everything I was doing didn't turn out as planned, regardless of how hard I tried. I felt I was doing the right things with the right amount of effort, but the dice just didn't roll my way.

Looking back at every one of my failures, I can say with 110% certainty that the reason I failed was because of my attitude and my effort.

There was a time in my life when I made terrible financial decisions, leading to my filing for bankruptcy back in the early 1990s. It was a difficult lesson, but one I wouldn't trade for anything in the world. Without this failure, I wouldn't have been able to lay the groundwork for future successes and accomplishments. I had to take responsibility for my bad decisions and live with the consequences.

Hitting the bottom does teach us many lessons, one of which is not wanting to be there ever again!

Potential alone isn't enough. Taking responsibility is the match that sets passion ablaze. We must have a better attitude in life so passion can arise from the depths of our guts to fill out every cell of our being. Conversely, a bad, negative, and pessimistic attitude kills passion and needs to be exterminated ASAP.

Uncaring people with bad attitudes are always unhappy, but they can't understand why. Do you know anyone with that kind of mentality? If this is you, YOU NEED TO STOP.

To live the life of a UE, you must avoid becoming stagnant, inactive, and prevent yourself from getting a terminal case of "bad attitude." If you've lost the joy on your life's journey, maybe it's because you've allowed a bad attitude to creep into your headspace. You must take responsibility.

Attitude is much more important than your background, education, money, failures, successes, or what other people think, say, or do. If all but one of the strings on your guitar is broken, then all you can do is play on that one string that's left: your attitude. Life is 5% what happens to us, and 95% how we react to it.

How prepared are you to meet adversity? What percentages would you use to describe how you react to circumstances?

Moreover, it's very easy for us to fall into that old trap of getting caught up in the daily grind of working all of the time, which sucks up the energy, time, and motivation to enjoy happy moments we feel we're owed, such as daydreaming.

Private Time

Spending time with nobody else around is the foundation of all successful entrepreneurs, regardless of the industry that they are involved in. Without private time, you will find it impossible to realize your full potential and set yourself on the path that leads to the proper work/life balance.

When I need a jolt of creative electricity, I go to the mountains in Montana. Simple things like listening to the sounds of the wind dancing through the tall trees, watching the morning mist rise from the wet grass and river, and building a campfire while having a good cup of coffee are euphoric and revitalizing to me.

There are trees and rivers in every corner of the country, but Montana has a special power over my soul. My stepfather Pat and my mother bought property there back in the 1990s. It is a nurturing place where I feel most at home, regardless of where I live.

Mother Nature is the battery for my soul. I can easily get in touch with myself very quickly in her midst. Regardless of what is going on in my life, she always puts things back in order and gives me the proper perspective to solve many of life's challenges.

Where do you go to recharge?

Life's Great Lesson

One day, a millionaire businessman took his son to the country to show him how the poor folks lived. They spent a few days on a farm with an extremely poor family. After they returned home, the father asked his son what he thought of his experience.

"It was great, Dad," the son replied.

"Did you see how poor some people in this world are?" the father asked.

"I sure did. I saw that we have a dog, and they have four. We have a big pool in our backyard, and they have a lake and a stream running through theirs that has no end. In our garden, we have fancy imported Italian oil lamps, and they have a sky filled with the stars. Our patio reaches all around to our front porch, and they have the entire horizon. Thank you, Dad, for showing me what true riches are."

Some people think that their value as a human being comes from working long hours, driving big expensive cars, dropping fifty thousand dollars on a vacation, and having lots of bling.

Me, I'm more of a BBQ on the back deck, guitar in the corner, hanging out in the mountains, reading a good business book, and playing with my kids kinda guy. That's not to say that I don't enjoy the finer things in life, but we all need to stick to our core values and beliefs.

Designing and creating your perfect lifestyle may take some serious brainstorming and redefining what is tremendously important, and some rearranging of your current priorities. You may need to completely break things down into the absolute smallest pieces, then rebuild your thinking with fewer moving parts.

Realizing your dream life is not a one-time thing. It's a living and breathing organism that requires constant attention and mental energies.

Once that piece of the puzzle is on solid ground, it's time to work on our time management skill.

CHAPTER 11

Effective Time Management

I believe that each one of us wishes we had more time in our days. On Friday afternoon, we are filled with excitement about all the wonderful things we will accomplish on the weekend, then Sunday night rolls around and we wonder where the weekend went.

There are two types of people on this planet: Those who squander their time, and those who make every second count.

The first type simply waits for the time to pass. For them, the time-lapse is often an annoyance. The example is anxiously waiting for the working hours to pass.

The second type makes every passing second count. Instead of just waiting for the sand to slip through the narrow funnel, they live with almost a pathological intent and never allow time to pass unnoticed. For them, the time-lapse is a living process, and they always strive to be active participants in it.

Effective time management is the one thing that separates top performers from the herd and allows them to reach higher ground. There's

There's a profound difference between time management and not caring about anything else beyond the current interest. And while we've developed a neat way to track time, it's beyond our capabilities to absolutely control it. However, we can induce a necessary level of control over the chaos of our lives. This means controlling our most precious asset, time, to the best of our abilities.

We cannot earn more of it or save it as we do with money or commodities. It is slipping away with every breath we take. The only thing we can do, in between our breaths, is control how and on what we are spending that time.

The 80/20 Principle

When you choose to stay focused on one single task at a time, you invariably end up cutting out some things you enjoy that may not be bearing fruit. We will do an exercise to help you eliminate, automate, or delegate up to 80% of your daily tasks and free your time and energy to dedicate to your superpowers.

Most people have heard of the Pareto 80/20 Principle, which suggests that 80% of your outcomes are from 20% of your efforts. Conversely, 20% of your outcomes are from the other 80% of your efforts. The point here? Identifying a group of top priorities and staying focused on them should be your number one focus. I want you to think about what activities in your day produce the most positive results in your business or personal life.

Earlier in my entrepreneurial career, I made a living in the world of professional photography and became an instructor traveling the world teaching the finer points of business. Today, it seems like everybody, and their brother's friend's aunt's sister, is now a "photographer," which has put a big crunch on those who have been professionally trained. Weekend warriors and soccer moms have taken the industry by storm with their $500 cameras and smartphones.

Professional photographers are married to their computers and workflows. Image processing that used to be handled by professional color labs is now being done by the photographers themselves, adding significantly more hours to their already long work week.

In photography, only three things make money: shooting, selling, and marketing. That's it! Retouching a digital file doesn't fall under any of those categories, but this digital process is consuming many pros. Why? Because they think it saves money, and they know how to do it. A deadly combination.

It's easy for us to dispose of things we dread and despise, but what about the things we're attached to? This makes it a lot harder because our emotions are involved. Photographers who spend eight hours on a Sunday editing and retouching files from Saturday's wedding are attached to an outdated method of running a business. In the open market, the job of a digital retoucher is $15-$20/hour. If a professional photographer were asked if they would be willing to work for $15-$20/hour, they would laugh in your face! Well, if they are doing their own retouching...

Instead of outsourcing the job to someone to free up their valuable time, they choose to do it themselves because they're emotionally attached to the digital process, or mistakenly think they're saving money.

In business today, there are 3 levels to what I call the "Time Value Pyramid":

- $15-$20/Hr. - The tasks that keep your business moving forward like answering the phone, responding to e-mails, processing orders, assembling products, etc.

- $50/Hr. - The day-to-day management of your business, setting sales goals and objectives, personnel management, and training, etc.

- $500/Hr. - Constructing the long-range goals of the company, creating the broad strokes, and crafting the overall vision. This is where *YOU* should be spending most of your precious time.

I can tell you this without any hesitation. Doing $15-$20 worth of work per hour is NOT what business owners should be doing with their time, whatever industry they're in!

Do you have a list of tasks that can be delegated or eliminated from your routine? Think about that.

This way of thinking may challenge the way you're used to running your business, but I can tell you that your business will be revolutionized by quantum leaps if you begin to entertain the idea of redesigning your thought processes.

The POD System

The way I do it is with what I call the POD system. Every activity is entered into a category, assigned a block of time, and placed on my schedule.

One trick that I always do at the end of each week is to sit down and plan the following week. I have some things that are in my schedule book for weeks and months in advance, but the day-to-day tasks that are necessary to keep the ship afloat are where the ultimate success lies.

On Monday morning, I have my game plan already in place and can be much more productive than simply allowing the wind to dictate where my time is spent.

For example, the first two hours of my day are always *"Mitche time."* This includes listening to music or a podcast, reading a book, drinking a good cup of coffee, and reviewing my goals for the day.

This POD of time is blocked off in my schedule book. I don't allow anything to interrupt me during this time. I make sure I do not get distracted by email, texts, social media timelines, notifications, and so on.

It's important that this first POD of the day be completely controlled by you and that you're not reacting to anything the world is dishing out.

Next, in the Family POD, I get the kids fed, ready, and bussed off to school. After that, the Reactive POD consists of replying to emails, returning phone calls, and anything else the world needs from me.

In the Revenue POD, I have a pre-defined list of objectives written down ahead of time.

After this work POD, it's back to either a personal or family POD to finish off the day. If you were to look at my schedule book, you would see a series of blocked out sections that are dedicated time slots for that activity. I'm not successful all the time, but I've developed a strong sense of purpose when it comes to sticking to my guns over the years.

This strategy is dependent upon asserting your ability to keep outside influences from interrupting you. If you're in the middle of your personal POD, don't spend time on your phone looking at work emails or checking online orders. If you're in your Revenue POD, don't allow yourself to be distracted by checking your Facebook timeline or looking up a recipe for tonight's dessert.

It's like putting out a virtual *"DO NOT DISTURB"* sign around your brain, then working like crazy to stay on the course. Always keep in mind the "nagging" question: Does this activity or task help me attain my ultimate lifestyle goals? Utilize the POD System in a scheduling app and don't forget to limit their duration. Continue by adding everything else you might plan for that day.

In the evening, take a few moments and rewind your day. See what you've missed. See what you've miscalculated.

Recall all those seemingly insignificant events you failed to predict that caused time losses. After a while, you'll start noticing how a vast number of such events repeat themselves day after day. To become a master of your schedule, you will need to be laser-focused on the most important tasks that bring the biggest results: Your own 80/20 list.

Delegate, Eliminate, Automate.

Meet my long-time friend, Bob. He's an entrepreneur who started out doing things the hard way, but then turned smart instead. We'll use him as a real-life example of how a single man can disrupt a global paradigm.

Just like you, Bob always dreamed of owning his own business. Eventually, he quit his job and invested some money into starting his professional lawn care company. He purchased a new lawnmower, rakes, wheelbarrows, gloves, and other items needed to be successful with his new venture. At that point, Bob was the only employee and in charge of not only mowing all the lawns, but also marketing, networking, sales, website design, payables, and other tasks.

To his own surprise, Bob managed to pick up several clients over a short time and eventually nearly filled up his schedule with recurring jobs every week. Not bad for a new business, but Bob knew how to work hard and smart.

One day, he received a call from the local shopping mall asking if he'd be interested in taking over the contract for their landscape maintenance.

After meeting with management, Bob figured that he would need to spend nearly all his time during the week at the mall just to fulfill the contract. That meant that all his other clients would have to wait.

On the flip side, the contract would exactly double his weekly revenue, so Bob had a hard time with the decision. Let's say there is a big hopper or vat that has three different sections: Delegation, Elimination, and Automation.

For the sake of the argument, let's put Bob's new opportunity into the hopper.

- Can Bob **delegate** the job to someone else? He could potentially hire a new employee to handle only the mall contract or handle private residence contracts. That's certainly a possibility.

- Can he simply turn down the contract and **eliminate** the possibility altogether? Absolutely. But it depends on what Bob's ultimate goals are for growing his business.

- Can he streamline and **automate** the task? Bob could purchase a larger lawnmower allowing him to finish his jobs much quicker, thus freeing up valuable time to handle more work. Great possibility!

When Bob sat down to look at all his options, he remembered that his ultimate goal was to expand his business and hire employees, which would give him more time to grow the business.

Most importantly, this strategy would give him more time to spend with his family.

Hence, Bob decided to bring on another employee and purchased a bigger lawnmower to handle the larger jobs. This freed up more time and allowed him to pick up five more commercial contracts.

The bottom line is that asking straightforward questions can potentially revolutionize your business. Therefore, give yourself the creative freedom and passion to think out-of-the-box. You'll be amazed at what can transpire!

Today, Bob lives and works his version of the 24/7 Lifestyle, and just like you should, he loves every moment of it.

The 4X Formula

By automating, delegating, and eliminating your daily tasks in an uber-efficient way, you will be able to free up a substantial amount of time in your day. This time can be reinvested into the 20% of your tasks that bring you 80% of your positive results or can be spent doing other things. It's your choice.

Basically, you will be able to get twice as much done in ½ the amount of time. I called this "4Xing" your life! It's a very straightforward and simple formula, but one will require constant attention if you are going to become a master.

In fact, I believe that with all of the modern day efficiencies and tools, the 80/20 has really become more like a 95/5. 95% of our results come from the 5% of our daily activities that truly move the needle on our lives. If you can keep that in your mind during the day, it will have a dramatic effect on your productivity, I can guarantee it!

The 1st Component – MENTAL IMAGERY

Mental imagery is a neat mind trick that enables us to predict up to 90% of events in the hours, days, weeks, and years ahead. In other words, it allows you to plan to perfection even over the large time gaps. It's something frequently used by top athletes, military strategists, and top executives.

How does it work?

When he was still a young athlete, Olympic gold-medalist Michael Phelps had real difficulties concentrating. He was built for the swimming pool but didn't yet have a champion mentality. A long, flat torso with long and strong arms on relatively short legs made him exceptionally hydrodynamic. But his inability to focus frustrated Phelps.

To solve this severe issue, his trainer designed a two-part mental workout that would ultimately make Michael Phelps the fastest swimmer in the world.

In the first phase, Michael was tasked to memorize every moment of the training and then rewind the mental movie afterward. Day after day, Phelps would teach his brain to remember more and more details about strokes, turns, energy levels, and duration. In less than six months, Phelps could remember details. He was even able to analyze the dynamics with surgical precision.

Then came phase two where Michael was supposed to plan his own training ahead of time, using his memories as the foundation. Once on the edge of a swimming pool, Phelps would play the mental movie and then jump in the water.

With practice, he learned to accurately assess the duration of the race down to the second. His brain would calculate the needed energy investment for every stroke so he could perfectly balance the reserves. Only a year after that, Phelps became the fastest male swimmer in his age category. Three years later, he broke several world records and won his first gold medal.

To a large extent, Phelps' secret was the ability of the human brain to act as a learning machine. Just as you can develop a habit, you can teach your brain to execute complex tasks basically on autopilot. Those tasks soon transform into habits.

The 2nd Component – THE IVY LEE METHOD

So many young executives are bragging about their multitasking abilities. There must be something to it, right?

Only chaos, confusion, and underachieving. Multitasking and micromanaging are the two capital mistakes in business operations. To an experienced eye, they are indicative of an inexperienced person or, at the very least, someone who's biting far more than he's capable of chewing.

Multi-taskers experience frequent burnouts, which negatively affects their overall efficiency.

Back in the 1920s, one man developed the single most efficient method of prioritizing that is in use even today.

Ivy Lee was hired to coach the executives of American Steel magnate Charles M. Schwab. Lee advised Schwab's managers to list only six tasks for the following day according to their priorities. They were expected to work on completing those tasks in the allotted time without proceeding to the next task unless the current one was finished. Today, most successful managers are using Ivy Lee's Method of prioritizing when creating a schedule.

Why only six? And what happens if we fail to execute all six planned for a given day? You simply move the unfinished tasks to the next day and fill in the remaining spots until there are exactly six tasks.

There's only so much you can fit into a single working day and still maintain a high level of quality. If you often find yourself in a situation where there are more than six tasks to complete, that probably indicates that you're micromanaging. Six is the sweet spot. Simple as that. If you were to compare your list of six things, I bet it would be close to the 80/20 exercise you did earlier!

Now, imagine the combo of mental imagery and Ivy Lee's Method of prioritizing in planning anything you can think of, especially time management...

The 3rd Component – PRACTICAL APPLICATION

The biggest challenge in time management is not planning and organizing a schedule, it's dealing with time vampires that chip away at your list of priorities and waste minutes and hours of your day. Some of this is not our fault, but most of it is. We make decisions throughout our day that allow our focus to be broken, and our important tasks delayed.

Two Types Of Schedules

One manages your private life. The other manages professional tasks. Here's the trick.

Tasks must be organized in a way that allows for so-called power-scheduling. We'll do a little exercise soon to teach you what power-scheduling truly is.

Now, the key here is not merely listing tasks. You also need to limit the duration of each task to save time. If you are having a scheduled meeting, that event must have both a start and end time, and you shouldn't exceed it unless necessary.

That's what makes Ivy Lee's Method so powerful. Once you get used to it, it will become increasingly easy to ditch everything that has lower significance in terms of a priority.

This is also the moment when that thin line between alleged "time management" and just not caring is crossed. Another brilliant feature of Ivy Lee's Method.

Sometimes, an idea may occupy your entire being. It becomes virtually impossible to shake it off. What do you do in such a situation?

EXERCISE: Power-Scheduling

Power-Scheduling refers to creating and managing a private schedule and a professional one. How do you do it efficiently? By combining mental imagery and Ivy Lee's Method of prioritizing.

Close your eyes for a couple of minutes and visualize the day ahead. Direct a mental movie of your day.

Start by imagining well-known, fixed-time events. Remember, there's only so much that you can't predict when you put your mind into it. For the most part, your days are following the same rut that is based on a set of habits you developed over the course of time. Your habits simply fit in those of your private and professional environments.

I believe that if you focus on the most important tasks and automate, delegate, or eliminate everything else, you will completely revolutionize the way your business operates. You will suddenly find that you have extra time in your day, and from there you can choose what to do with it.

Perhaps invest it back into growing your business, looking for new opportunities, or taking your family on a picnic. The sky is the limit!

CHAPTER 12

It's A Wrap

Well, there you have it.

You have navigated through the digital jungle of our societal addiction to our devices, designed the perfect life, and reshuffled your priorities on how you spend your time. All in about a week, not bad I would say!

The journey you are now going to embark on will undoubtedly be filled with ebbs and flows, but in the long run will give you the ultimate control of how you spend your time, whether you choose to be on your phone, fishing for trout on a mountain stream, or playing a game of Sky Dragon in the backyard.

Living in the moment is all any of us have. We don't know what the next moment will bring, so by golly we had better make sure to make the most of THIS moment.

You have decided to spend a few of your moments with me, and for that I am eternally grateful.

I wish you luck with your new set of eyes!

Sources:

Rothberg, M. B., Arora, A., Hermann, J., Kleppel, R., St. Marie, P., & Visintainer, P. (2010). Phantom vibration syndrome among medical staff: a cross-sectional survey. BMJ, 341, c6914. doi:10.1136/bmj.c6914. Available at: https://www.bmj.com/content/341/bmj.c6914

https://breakthemindset.com/top-10-ways-to-reduce-digital-distractions/

https://gradesfixer.com/free-essay-examples/who-am-i-in-the-digital-world-paradox-of-digital-communication/

https://neighborsc.org/the-paradox-of-digital-wellbeing/

https://edition.cnn.com/2017/05/19/health/instagram-worst-social-network-app-young-people-mental-health/index.html#:~:text=Instagram%20is%20the%20most%20detrimental,Public%20Health%20in%20the%20UK.

https://www.rsph.org.uk/static/uploaded/d125b27c-0b62-41c5-a2c0155a8887cd01.pdf

https://www.psychologytoday.com/us/blog/insight-therapy/202305/face-to-face-communication-healthier-than-digital

https://www.sciencedirect.com/science/article/pii/S2451958821000361

https://www.betterup.com/blog/face-to-face-communication

https://www.independent.co.uk/tech/employees-b2474694.html

https://www.hrpolicy.org/insight-and-research/resources/2024/01/member-only/01/smartphone-access-may-help-reduce-stress-and-impro/

https://www.qualtrics.com/blog/phones-affect-work-life-balance/

https://www.flashhub.io/what-is-the-productivity-paradox/

https://nomophobia.com/blog/the-productivity-paradox-how-to-harness-the-power-of-technology-without-burnout/

https://medium.com/illumination/the-productivity-paradox-how-smart-people-are-fooling-themselves-50c858e0b861

https://www.linkedin.com/pulse/paradox-productivity-apps-how-can-make-you-less-more-stressed-amjad-zem8f/

https://www.forbes.com/advisor/car-insurance/texting-driving-statistics/

https://www.ncbi.nlm.nih.gov/pmc/articles/

Get A <u>FREE</u> Paperback Copy Of Mitche's Best-Selling Book That Revolutionized The Customer Experience!

**Get your FREE paperback at
www.PowerMarketing101.com/CS**

Download Your Copy of Mitche's FREE Report "5 Steps To Digital Detox"

Visit
www.PowerMarketing101.com/detox

www.ingramcontent.com/pod-product-compliance
Lightning Source LLC
LaVergne TN
LVHW051050080426
835508LV00019B/1803